A Marvellous Party

Foreword

On the morning of January 10 2015, as I woke to the shattering news that David Bowie had died, I did what most people in the world did, and posted my feelings on Facebook.

Just the one word. *Inconsolable.*

But I added something particular to my post, something which always fills me with a heady cocktail of pride, wonder and disbelief every time I look at it: a candid photograph of David Bowie, rock legend, cultural icon and my absolute and ultimate hero... and I am standing beside him.

There are those who say that you should never meet your heroes, for fear of disappointment. I say they are wrong. I met all the heroes and heroines that I have written about in this book, which might prompt some sour-faced meanies to brand me as a groupie, a stalker, a *mad fan* or – maybe – a bit sad.

I call myself extremely lucky.

Some of the encounters were accidental, some were orchestrated, some were professional, and some were personal. Most of them were brief, all of them were memorable and none of them were remotely disappointing. And after every single one, all I could think was

How the hell did that happen?

A Marvellous Party

Ian Elmslie

Ignite Books

ISBN: 978-0-9932044-2-5

cover design by Nik & Tom at bookbeaver.co.uk
typeset by Steve at Ignite.
www.ignitebooks.co.uk

Printed and bound by
CPI Group (UK) Ltd,
Croydon. CR0 4YY

With love and gratitude to all the guests,
to those who left the party too soon,
and to those who stayed until after the end.

xx

Contents

Prologue: when a fairy hits fifty

On July 27 1967 I was five years old, The Beatles were at number one with *All You Need Is Love* and homosexuality was decriminalised. A big day for all concerned.

Fifty years. A lot has happened since then.

Funny age, fifty. If life begins at forty, what happens when you hit a half-century? Letters start to arrive from insurance companies offering you life insurance policies and inviting you to consider a pension plan. You tend to plump for a package holiday or an all-inclusive cruise rather than going backpacking and sleeping in a beach hut. Any concert, sporting event or occasion that requires you to stand for the entire duration is now not an option.

You grow hair where you don't want it, lose it where you do, and what were once natural highlights are now resolutely grey.

You cleanse, tone and moisturise yourself into a stupor, and it doesn't make a buggery bit of difference to anything but your bank balance. An invitation to a party now invariably means a dinner party, with a prompt 7.30 start and carriages at midnight, as opposed to a drunken bop on a crisp-encrusted carpet into the early cold pizza hours of morning.

Parts of your body start to ache and click like chopsticks, the bathroom cabinet is rammed with creams that heat and gels that freeze, and it takes a little longer to get off the sofa.

You now go to bed at the same time you used to go out. The working day dominates the week, the household chores rule the weekend, and the Sunday grumps set in just as *Songs of Praise* is firing up your inner atheist.

But – in spite of all this inevitable slide into senility – you are now officially entitled to start the majority of your stories with the words *I remember...*

Just like growing a beard and getting a tattoo, it would appear that it is now essential for every gay man to celebrate hitting his fifties by writing a memoir. A homossential, as 'twere.

We can't blame this trend on a mid-life crisis because, if we pay heed to the law of averages, mid-life was around ten years ago, and in the gay world, which spins twice as quickly, we're probably talking the day you hit twenty-five. So, instead, let's call fifty a time to pause for thought, a stop-gap, a moment to reflect on the ride so far, a chance to acknowledge where we've been, what we've done and recline in a scented bathtub of our own memories.

We all have stories to share, those well-worn tales we have tried, tested and told over the dinner table to amuse and possibly impress others. And oh, how we love to glean out *the good bits*, separating the wheat from the chaff, and aim our moment in the candlelight fairly and squarely at the funny bone, with the occasional assault on the tear ducts.

The stories I have chosen to share with you are no more and no less funny, moving, fascinating or unique than your own.

But they are *my* stories. Stories from my childhood, my teenage years, my professional and personal life, a gay man's journey from there to here.

Interwoven with these reminiscent observations of places and faces that all became pieces in the puzzle, I wish to pay tribute to the men and women who threw down a trail of breadcrumbs to guide, encourage, and inspire me along the way.

My heroes.

Heroes. We've all got them. They might be a much-missed grandparent, who entranced us with stories of air-raids and dripping sandwiches, or parents who loved us absolutely and unconditionally, or an older sibling who let us play, fight, love, loathe and learn from them, or a best friend, the one who, to this day, still calls to see if you are coming out to play. It could be a pop star, one of those smiling or sultry faces we pinned to our walls, wearing out their paper lips as we kissed them good-night, whose eyes made us swoon or whose bony fingers pointed out through the television screen and summoned us to think outside of our bedrooms and join their gang.

Maybe a sportsman, the captain carried aloft on his team mates' shoulders, brandishing the cup of victory, the one who ran the fastest or jumped the highest, or a tennis champion, clambering over the seats to embrace their loved one at the moment of triumph. They could be a writer, whose words transported us from our humdrum lives into exciting wonder-lands, or a comedian who made us laugh till our stomachs ached and the tears of joy rolled down our faces.

Actors, film stars, artists, poets, politicians, kings, queens… or someone, anyone, a nobody but a somebody who shone a torch to guide you through the darkest hours of self-doubt, loneliness, confusion, grief, and led you to the light.

It's your call.

As a gay boy – and later, man – born in the Sixties, a teenager in the Seventies, and then released into the working world in the Eighties, I was constantly looking for clues as to who I was, who I could be, where I could go, and what I could do with my life.

I found the answers in music, in films, in books, in theatres and on television, and steadily pieced together an outfit that has clothed, defined and protected me ever since. And, by beautiful and occasionally surreal twists of fate, I have been lucky enough to have usually brief but close encounters with many of the men and women who fired my imagination, opened the doors, shone the light and gave me permission to follow a dream and live my life. Many of these encounters occurred during the Nineties, when I was one half of a cabaret act called Katrina and the Boy, and it is recollections from those years that form the centrepiece of this book.

We were regular performers on the largely unknown gay cabaret circuit, a grubby and glitzy world of home-sewn glamour and bawdy gags, of sky-scraping wigs and wicked wit, of foul-mouthed drag queens, baby-oiled strippers, leathered and laced disco divas and anyone else who had the guts to get up in front of the toughest audience in the world. Because let's face it, when you're working in front of a crowd of queens, half of them are thinking *It should be me up there*.

The Nineties were a pivotal era in the history of the gay community. While we should have been celebrating a new and welcome visibility in the outside world, far removed from the archaic ignorance and bigotry of the not-too-distant past, we found ourself not only fighting for our rights, but also for our lives. Our increasingly liberated lifestyle was under attack from government policies, which threatened to drive us back down and underground. We were also battling a disease that was running rampant, with no treatments and no cure, and which was killing our friends on a weekly basis.

But, when the going gets tough, the tough get singing, dancing, marching, shouting, fighting, crying when we must, and laughing when we choose.

From my vantage point on various stages up, down, and across the country, I observed and hopefully entertained my community during these challenging yet glorious years, and I remain honoured and proud to have been right at the centre of both the celebration and the fight for survival.

My book is about my journey, and the people I found by chance and whom I chose to help me along the way. Some are famous, some are very famous, some are still alive, some have passed, and there are some – like me – who you will never have heard of before.

It is not a strictly chronological autobiography, and I beg your indulgence and forgiveness as I flit from thought to thought. Random recollections, it's a fifty thing. Kinda like CD shuffle.

As I finished writing and considered a title, I realised that my life has felt like being a guest at a marvellous party. I was never the host, and only occasionally, by virtue of a spotlight, the centre of attention.

Indeed, I have spent most of the time willingly standing in the shadows, watching and wondering how the hell was I blessed with the good fortune to be sharing a moment in such stellar company, and to have the opportunity to thank them for that handful of breadcrumbs.

They were private moments, not played out on stages or screens, but backstage, in dressing rooms, at parties, where there were no cameras and when the sometimes unforgiving glare of the spotlight was turned off, and I was allowed to share a few precious minutes with the private person behind the public image.

I am delighted to report that I was never once disappointed. Indeed, I was always touched by their bemused humility that someone should think so much of them.

We never know how many lives we touch until we are lucky enough to be told.

If my ramblings amuse you, I hope that you are encouraged to recall and tell *your* stories, share them with friends and with the world, acknowledge your heroes, and realise that, maybe, to someone…

You are a hero.

Young love

The day I met
Donny Osmond

Young love, first love

His dark brown eyes look directly into mine, his face sympathetic, without that famous trademark smile, and his voice is quiet and genuinely concerned.

Those same eyes that once stared out from every inch of my bedroom wall, the same face that was featured on the sleeve of the very first record I ever bought, and that same voice, the one that had sung the songs that taught me about love. *Young love, first love.*

It wasn't the first time we had met, but we weren't what anyone could call friends. I was maybe more than 'just another fan', probably because I am a man – and a male Donny Osmond fan will always be as rare as a vegetarian in a steak house.

But – whether fan or friend – here I am, almost thirty years after three minutes of pop changed my life, being comforted by my pre-teen idol over the loss of my father.

And they called it puppy love…

I wonder…when and how do we learn about love?

When I was five, my down-the-road 'girlfriend' Jacqueline had given me a book called *What Colour is Love?* about flowers of different colours and animals of different breeds who live side by side and get along with each other, and how people, sometimes, manage to do the same. Quite radical and right-on for a five-year-old girl from Surrey.

But love was just a word that I put at the bottom of a *thank you* letter to a kindly aunt or grandmother, written the day after my birthday or on Boxing Day. I had certainly seen pieces of theatre and film where love was an element, but it was usually between some Aristocats or a prince and a princess, so it meant next to nothing to me. I wasn't repulsed by it. I certainly didn't find it *yukky*. I just didn't understand it.

My parents were not the most demonstrative of people when it came to displays of affection, either with each other or with their children. My Dad was often away on business for days at a time, and Mum ran the household to a strict timetable. There was an overriding atmosphere of formality, and it saddens me that I cannot remember many moments of shared laughter, or being lost in the warmth of a cuddle. Something was missing. I just didn't know what.

I wonder…how does a young gay boy learn about love?

We are given no clues, no guidance, no indication about how to deal with the feelings that are steadily rising within us, which – we are simultaneously being informed by our peers, our teachers and parents, and maybe even by our own young minds – are not only wrong, and disgusting, but also a one-way ticket to eternal damnation and hell.

Where do we look? Who do we turn to?

Someone help me, help me, help me please...

During the school holidays, I was sent for tennis and swimming lessons, as both a physical and a social exercise. My swimming teacher looked like George Best, which was considered pretty damn handsome at the time. Even though I had no interest in football, I knew all about E for B and Georgie B. Everyone knew George Best.

My teacher was dark, handsome and as hairy as a bear, and with a physique that befitted his profession. One day, a fellow pupil decided to push me into the deep end of the pool, which prompted my teacher to swim over and save one very distressed but barely drowning little lad.

As he pulled me up from the water, I threw my arms around his neck and nestled my face into his chest, gasping for air, crying, and scared to death. I felt his fur against my cheek, and his muscled arm around me, and he let me stay there until I was calm and comforted.

And I thought...*I am very happy here.*
I dreamt about him that night.
And that's when I knew. For sure. *I knew.*

But I still needed a clue as how to put this feeling into words. And then, one afternoon, I heard it. I was watching television. I cannot remember the programme, the day of the week, or any other detail. But I do remember a field of daffodils, with a dark haired boy, in a floral-patterned shirt, seated and almost lost amongst the flowers.

And they called it puppy love...

The song was a broken-hearted ballad, richly orchestrated, punctuated with repeated and impassioned pleas for help and prayers for someone to be *back in my arms once again...*

I had no idea what *puppy love* was, I wasn't *in my teens* and the concept of loving *her* was already a distinct impossibility. This song should have had no effect on me at all, but...

Someone help me, help me,
help me please...

This song was about love. Love that you couldn't have, but love that you wanted so badly. Love that others didn't understand. Love that caused you pain and almost unbearable heartache. Love that seemed hopeless. But love you believed would someday happen, and love that would last forever.

The singer of this song was Donny Osmond.

For my birthday, I received my very own transistor radio, and the whole world of pop music opened up. From the moment I woke up, my radio was on, tuned to *Radio One*, and I soaked up all the songs of the day, listening out for another play of something by Donny Osmond.

My patience was rewarded by the release of *Too Young* which was even better than *Puppy Love*. My mother, smugly, told me that it was a song popular *in her day*, but that didn't matter. It was all new to me.

In the August holiday of that year, with my father driving over the Pyrenees, I sat in the back seat, singing *Puppy Love* on an endless loop and driving everyone to the point of stopping the car and hurling me down the mountainside.

As if announcing my dream of being a ballet dancer to my playground peers wasn't reckless enough, I compounded the deal by declaring my admiration for Donny Osmond, once again ensuring a flurry of well-aimed blows and juvenile insinuations about my masculinity.

It was so clear to every other lad on the playground what you should do, what you should say and what you should like.

Boys read *Shoot*, girls read *Bunty*. Boys watched *The Tomorrow People*, girls watched *Follyfoot*. Boys liked The Sweet, Slade, Alice Cooper and Gary Glitter. Girls liked Donny Osmond.

So, it's official. Elmslie's a girl.

I'm not sure how I coped with it, but cope with it I did.

Christmas 1972, and amongst the traditional presents were two seven-inch singles, *Ben* by Michael Jackson, and *Why* by Donny Osmond, the latter wrapped in a sleeve of blue and yellow, with a lion's head and the grand lettering of MGM emblazoned upon it.

If this wasn't enough, as I sat on a carpet of wrapping paper, digesting the seasonal blowout and waiting for the compulsory viewing of The Queen's Speech, there he was on *Top Of The Pops* singing my Christmas present, just for me.

Purple shirt, white waistcoat, shiny dark brown hair, gleaming white teeth, and brown eyes framed by long lashes...

And here I have to state categorically, that I never, ever ever, fancied Donny Osmond. *Ever.* He was undeniably attractive, but in a pop world starred by Gilbert O'Sullivan and Peter Skellern, the competition – with the possible exception of the feather-haired and undeniably pretty David Cassidy – was not too fierce. No, it was the music and only the music for me. The songs weren't about sex, they were about love. There were no gutsy guitars, no pounding drums, no screaming vocals.

Maybe it was merely a tentative step up from the ballet scores and musicals that I knew so well and loved so much. Maybe it was the strings, and the honey-sweet harmonies which created this warm cloud of lovely feelings that I could not articulate, but that I knew that I liked.

Why? Because I love you.

Owning a 7-inch single was like eating one Pringle. It was never going to be enough. My brother and I never received pocket money, but we did receive a pound every year on our birthdays and at Christmas. The money was banked with Dad and the amount was noted inside the accompanying card.

Even though it was my money, I always felt very awkward about asking to make a withdrawal, and no more so than when I had the following conversation…

Dad, may I have £2.10 out of my Christmas money?
Why?
I want to buy a record.
What record?
A Donny Osmond record.
Why do you want it?
Because I really like it.
Are you sure you want it?

By this time, we were one cushion away from *Monty Python and the Spanish Inquisition*, but I held my nerve, got my money, and joined my mother on her next visit to neighbouring Reigate and steered her into *Rhythm*, the local record shop.

Rhythm was very respectable, predominantly stocking classical collections, the easy listening of James Last and Bert Kaempfert, albums by the Wakiki Beach Boys and Nana Mouskouri for the package-holiday jet-setters, Val Doonican for the grans, and the tight-trousered Tom Jones for the ever-so-slightly desperate housewives. There was a cursory section holding the best-selling rock and pop records, and buried between Pink Floyd and Black Sabbath was the object of my desire.

Portrait of Donny. Two pounds and ten pence.
I lifted it out and beckoned my mother over to the till.

But, like every over-cautious parent, she wanted me to be sure that this was the one that I wanted and that I *really* wanted it. *Could you please read out the songs?* she asked the assistant, in her very best dinner party voice.

The lady behind the counter looked over her half-glasses, took a deep breath, and read out the tracks as if she were introducing debutantes at a coming-out ball. *Puppy Love...Hey Girl... Going Going Gone...I've Got Plans For You...*

I was squirming in my shoes and glowing with embarrassment as she read down the cover, until I blurted out

Yes, that's the one. That's it. Yes.

I duly handed over my money and headed home, vowing never to go record shopping with my Mum ever again. But it didn't matter now. The treasure had been found. I had my first album.

As I hit double figures, I steadily and surely retreated into my secret world. Doors that were usually left open were now firmly closed, and any intrusion into *my space* was an unwelcome disturbance.

As I locked myself away, with only my records for company, I began my studies in earnest. I listened to and learned every word, every note, every beat. I already had a rudimentary understanding of chords and melody lines from my weekly piano lessons, but here was a whole world of new fascinations.

I began to learn about arrangements, how strings can be used to great effect, when a song should lift with a crescendo and a key change.

I experienced a physical and emotional thrill when voices harmonised, and there was no-one who created that warm wall of sound better than The Osmonds. Oh yes, The Osmonds, as in the group.

Up to this point, it had been Donny all the way. But a trip to the local newsagents, and the surrender of the princely sum of 15p, had furnished me with a glossy magazine, published by the Daily Mirror, called *The Fantastic Osmonds*, crammed with pictures, biographies, *likes and dislikes*, images of the entire family posing down London's Carnaby Street, on holiday in Hawaii, and at home in this place called Utah.

Even better, the magazine had a section devoted to a review of a concert, complete with a whole host of shots of the band, resplendent in fringed and studded white suits, open at the chest, with huge belt buckles and shiny white ankle boots, dancing themselves into a sweaty mess in front of rows of rows of girls.

Now these girls were not sitting down, quietly watching and politely applauding after each song. They were on their feet, reaching their arms out, screaming and weeping.

I was used to going to the theatre, and sitting in still silence, but the wild excitement generated by the performance and captured in these photographs fascinated me and I wanted to be part of it. All of it.

Two Donny albums down, and I was ready for the hard stuff.

I bought a copy of *Crazy Horses*.

It was certainly louder than a Donny album. At times it sounded not dissimilar to the bands that my brother admired, with guitar riffs, punchy drums and top of the register vocals. The title track had been a big hit, and the whinnying keyboard hook gave the haters something to latch onto and mock.

Some songs took a while to like, but that was the advantage of twelve-inch vinyl. The needle went down, and you worked your way through each track, so that even ones that were initially challenging became familiar, then favourites. You never skipped a song. You were in for the duration, and it paid off.

Swimming rewards at Morden Baths had always been in the shape of ballet records. Now – as I breathlessly completed my first ever length – I was straight out of the pool and practically driving my Dad to the record store to pick up a copy of *The Osmonds Live*, an album which captured that insane outpouring of screamed adoration that I had only seen in pictures.

I was no longer just interested. I was obsessed.

If my friends had elder sisters, I begged them for any Osmond posters from their teen magazines, which I then Blu-Tacked to the wall, turning my once respectable bedroom into something more like a dental surgery. Teeth, teeth, and more teeth.

The whole world of pop music opened up for me, and every possible minute of every day was spent falling deeper into my new love. But being in a gang of one is a lonely place to be. I wanted, even needed to be with others who felt like me.

On the back of an album sleeve, I found the address for the Osmonds Fan Club.

I sent off my SAE and was duly rewarded with a invitation from Maureen, the secretary, to join the club. Once more unto my birthday account I went, withdrew the necessary £1.20, bought a postal order and sent it off, and waited by the window every morning, willing the postman's van to pull into our drive.

After what seemed like a lifetime, my envelope arrived, and what treasures it held! A plastic wallet, with the Osmond logo on the front, my membership card and number, a badge informing the world that I was now an *official* member of the fan club, a small book containing a brief history and a discography, a list of merchandise, a four-page printed newsletter, with three printed stickers to use for subsequent newsletters. Not bad for just over a quid!

But, *excuse me*, what is a Mormon?

And how do I become one?

The celestial checklist demanded no artificial stimulants, no smoking, no alcohol, no drugs and no pre-marital sex, with the promised reward of your own planet for eternity after a mere lifetime of abstinence.

I didn't drink tea and coffee. I hated *Coca Cola*. Cigarettes stank. I had tried a sip of my Dad's Guinness, which tasted like a burnt toast milkshake. Sex, pre-marital or otherwise, was not on the cards, drugs were not a consideration, and who wouldn't want their own planet?

So, count me in, I'm a Mormon!

If you were a fan, a real fan, you had to sign up for the whole deal. You swore your allegiance and wore your colours with pride. For Donny, everything had to be purple. Shirts, socks, right down to your towel and toothbrush. I never owned a Donny pillowcase, but if I could have done, I would have done.

As my mother branded my growing obsession a waste of time and money, pulling out the old chestnut of *You'll grow out of it*, my father appeared to be quietly bemused. After all, he had been a member of the George Formby Appreciation Society in his youth. I wonder if he got a little stick of Blackpool rock and a complimentary ukulele when he signed up.

When the time came for me to own my very own record player to house in my bedroom, we headed off to the local Comet, and an Alba stereo system was duly purchased. I had never owned anything so big or so expensive, and I was both awestruck and enormously grateful. Having wired the plug and attached the speakers, it was time to try it out and – at my father's request – the first song played was *Puppy Love*.

I can still see him, standing in the doorway, watching me, gently smiling.

The new releases kept on coming, the publicity machine kept on rolling and my bank account took a hammering, but my addiction had to be regularly fed.

Look-In was ditched for *Music Star*, filled with pictures and hilariously fictitious stories with eye-grabbing titles: *The Day Donny Came To Tea!* I even splashed the princely sum of £2 on a red velvet Donny cap, though I am not certain that I ever plucked up the courage to wear it out of the house.

Not that I was going out much at all. Wherever I went, I just wanted to get back to my little corner of the world.

A friend's birthday trip to the cinema was merely interruption to my music time, and I even threw away a tennis match in a local competition because I knew there was a TV show where Donny would be singing *The Twelfth Of Never*, with his new deeper voice, while wearing a really unfortunate custard-yellow polo-neck jumper.

He was number one in the charts and everybody likes to back a winner, which may explain my last ditch attempt at being *one of the lads*. Leeds United were the hottest team in the land, and I decided that it would do no harm to pretend to be a supporter. I even had a mug embossed with their emblem for my morning milk. But this time, maybe for the last time, my mother was right. I did *grow out of it* in all of three weeks, and happily conceded that *one of the lads* I will never be.

Being a fan, whether it be of a pop star or football team, is rooted in the same soil. It's all about belief in something or someone, and belonging to a gang of people who feel the same.

Fan hysteria, whether it be screamed at a concert or at a football match, has been likened to a religious experience, that moment when an ecstasy takes over your entire being and you surrender to the overwhelming power of the source and object of your adoration.

You will your idols to succeed, whether it is up the charts or towards the goalposts, you defend them to your last breath, and you convince yourself that, as long as you believe, they will never let you down. And when you are part of a crowd, sharing that experience and that belief, there is a unique feeling of unity and strength. A kind of love.

You have found a family.

Only I was too young to be allowed to meet them.

I could only watch in envy as a news broadcast showed scenes of mass meltdown outside the Rainbow Theatre, when all two thousand tickets to an Osmond concert sold out in minutes, leaving eighteen thousand unlucky girls, all of whom had camped out overnight to secure a seat, sobbing unconsolably on the pavements of Finsbury Park.

I jealously read an article in the morning paper, telling the tale of twelve thousand screaming teens who descended on Heathrow airport to watch their favourite family get off a plane, wave and get into a waiting car, and who were in such a frenzy that they pushed and shoved until a wall collapsed, raining masonry and metal on the unfortunate souls below. The accompanying photographs captured the aftermath, of girls bloodied and weeping, being carried in the arms of policeman over the rubble of bricks.

God, I so wished I had been there.

Being an Osmond fan took guts, especially after the release of the truly execrable *Long-Haired Lover From Liverpool*, which gave the playground tormentors an arsenal of ammunition to hurl in my direction, but stubborn as I was and loyal as I am, I held my head high and learned to fight my corner with my tongue rather than my fists.

On a family holiday to Jersey in the August of 1974, my mettle was truly put to the test. Yes, for one week the BBC turned over an evening hour to the Osmond family, to do with as they wished.

Brilliant!

But, not so brilliant when you are staying in a hotel, where there is only one television for the guests in the entire building, and *The Osmonds* early evening programme coincided with *Crossroads*, the popular early evening soap opera on ITV, set in a shaky walled motel and remembered for some of the most dismal acting in the history of television. Many of we children of the Seventies are still haunted by Benny and his beanie and his unrequited love for Miss Diane.

Whatever its failings – and there were many – it had a fiercely devoted audience of ladies in their 60s, who were determined not to miss an episode. However, they had not figured on going to battle with an eleven-year-old Osmond fan.

The rule of the room was whoever got there first got to choose the channel. And these old girls learned pretty damn quickly that you have to get up pretty damn early to catch me napping. For five days, I held my ground, and sat in the front row, hearing and feeling the verbal knives being hurled into my young whippersnapper of a back.

What did I care?

Donny was singing *Are you lonesome tonight?* while being swung on a cherry picker over the heads of the adoring, scarf-waving, seat-wetting masses. He had also teamed up with Marie, which meant even more albums for me to buy. *Love Me For A Reason* was Number One in the charts, and all was right with the world.

My team were still *Top Of The Pops*.

Where did all the good times go?

It wasn't easy being twelve.

There were The Wombles, for starters. A furry pack of ecologically aware rodents who made the Teletubbies look like the anti-Christ.

But even worse than The Wombles were the Bay City Rollers, who were consistently hitting the Number One spot and the screams that were once exclusively saved for the Osmonds were getting stolen and thus decidedly softer.

As my idols slowly crumbled, so did the protection of my bedroom, and reality began to invade my four-walled world.

My parents decided that I should get used to being away from home, in preparation for my forthcoming five year sentence at a public school in Cheltenham, and I became a weekly boarder at my preparatory school.

Radios were strictly banned and I suffered severe musical withdrawal symptoms. I had become so accustomed to the sanctuary of my own space and the constant company of my record collection that five whole days and nights of strict school regulations and being forced to sleep in an eight bed dormitory were not a recipe for happiness.

To add to my woes, the day of judgement in the shape of the Common Entrance exam was looming, and the word on the report was that my prospects were not looking good.

The weekends at home became a hotbed of tension. The dreaded mark card, delivered on Friday and collating five days of test grades into one damning percentage, only served to underline that my academic achievements were on the baseline. Less than 75% meant no television, less than 65% meant a beating.

I lived in absolute fear of Fridays.

Tutors were employed to coach me through the mysteries of Maths and French, and I was ordered to spend most of the day face down over my school books, with no music. Many a cross word was said, and I was left in no doubt that failure to pass the entrance exam would be a matter of huge embarrassment for the family and a personal sentence to life as a dustman. Anything that I enjoyed was seen as a distraction, and right at the top of the hit list was The Osmonds.

I was never a naughty child. I was never rude to my teachers. I did well in the subjects that I was interested in, and tried my best in the subjects that I either didn't like or couldn't understand. No child responds well to threats and punishment, and schoolwork became a source of absolute fear of failure.

All the shouting and all the smacking was not going to make a blind bit of difference to my comprehension of Maths or Science, and being away from home at school – no matter how hateful it was – became a strange respite from a rapidly disintegrating relationship between myself and my parents.

No matter how many prizes I won for music or poetry, no matter how many pieces of art were displayed at school exhibitions, no matter how well I did in the school play, I was made to feel like a disappointment.

And by now I knew for a fact that I was gay, which I was painfully aware would be the final straw.

This was not going to end well.

But, I still had Donny. I still had The Osmonds. I still had something to believe in, something to cling to that was mine, for which I would have laid down and died.

Then something horrible happened.

Donny brought out a single, and I didn't really like it.

It was short. It was repetitive. It was a bit dull. Actually, it was very dull. It didn't do much in the charts. Well, at least we now had something in common. We were both failures.

Where did all the good times go?

Somehow, I passed my exam.

My parents were more relieved than proud. The family honour had been preserved. The line of Elmslies at Cheltenham College, begun over a century ago, would be unbroken. My Dad had throughly enjoyed his time there, and enjoyed all the benefits of success within that system. My brother was already there, and loving every minute of it.

Now it was my turn.

The message delivered by my father on that September night before the beginning of this new chapter was clear and cold. Whatever mess I had made of my education at prep school was not going to happen again.

If I thought being an *out* Osmond fan at preparatory school was a challenge, I learned that at public school it was tantamount to a death sentence. The corridors of the house where I was imprisoned thrummed to the sound of Led Zeppelin, Genesis, Yes, Supertramp, Deep Purple, and if I was to survive, I was going to have to take a vow of absolute silence, and keep my musical closet door firmly closed.

All through that first year, I held my tongue and kept my head down. Any magazines I bought were kept strictly out of sight, and I saved my record buying for the holidays.

But it seemed that everything was changing with my favourite group, and not for the better. One mediocre group effort was followed by Donny's dismal attempt at disco, which in turn led to a Christmas collection so saccharine that it should have come with a government health warning.

Donny and his sister Marie now had their own variety show on TV, which was toe-curlingly awful, with dreadful kooky comedy routines and a syrupy selection of songs that were way too country and nowhere near rock'n'roll. No thirteen-year-old, no matter how brave, wants to sing along to

> *A my name is Alice and my boyfriend's name is Andy,*
> *we come from Alabama and we like apples.*

Wham bam, no thank you ma'am.

It was now worse than feeling embarrassed by my heroes. I felt betrayed.

Time takes a cigarette

Having seen a picture of David Bowie in 1976, scarecrow-thin, with slicked back hair and a packet of Gitanes tucked stylishly in his waistcoat pocket, I decided my next footstep on the rite of teenage passage should be to start smoking.

I bought a packet of 20, for the outrageous price of 75 pence, and sat on the floor of a nearby park bandstand, which afforded a good vantage point for eagle-eyed teachers and butt-kissing prefects. I struck a match, lit the cigarette and inhaled, choking as the black tobacco burned a pathway down through my virgin lungs, making my head spin and my stomach lurch.

I'd never felt so cool in my life.

To add further insult to injury of my internal organs, the object of my unrequited love, while treating me to a very risky Sunday afternoon visit to a pub, sneaked a shot of vodka into my traditional orange juice. He could have handed me a glass of hemlock and I would have happily drunk it just to die in his arms, but the vodka was tasty enough to secure my one way ticket out of an eternity on my own personal planet.

1977. Punk was in its infancy and I was right there at the birth. I spiked my hair, wore my tie skinny side out and pinned a picture of the Sex Pistols on my study wall. Rebellion was stirring in my soul and spinning on my turntable.

I escaped from the confines of College whenever the opportunity arose, walking around the town, hanging out in *Driftin*, the one store which stocked and played a wide selection of punk and new wave records, and owned by the charismatic Roger, the saxophonist of The Fabulous Poodles. I spent hours in that shop, thumbing through racks of sleeves, listening to the exciting sounds coming out of the speakers. Dark sounds, dirty sounds, angry sounds. No harmonies here.

One afternoon in 1978, I was in one of the many newsagents that sold records. You could get records in the most unlikely shops in the late Seventies, pretty much anywhere that wasn't a shoe shop or a bank.

I found myself in the Osmonds section, and picked up a copy of a new Donny and Marie album, with the unfortunate title of *Goin' Coconuts*. I flipped it over, read down the tracks, looked at the cover, and put it back in the rack.

And we're done.

The love affair is over.

On the shelf

When love dies, there must be a period of separation. A time to rage and repair, to mourn and move on. Out with the old and in with the new.

And so it is with your first pop idol.

Their picture is eventually ripped from the bedroom wall and becomes the faded photograph that you destroy, the former favourite outfit that you clear out of your wardrobe and send to a charity shop, and the once best-beloved song that now makes you shudder and turn off the radio.

They become the boyfriend you are embarrassed to admit that you ever loved, the infatuation that you label as a mere folly of youth, the person you swear that you never ever want to see again as long as you live.

And then, after a while, maybe you can bear to face each other again and acknowledge that, for better or for worse, you will always be a part of each other's history.

In the Spring of 1987, I was in my final year at drama school. It had been an extraordinary, informative, rewarding and mostly happy time, but something had just gone terribly wrong.

I had learned a lot about life, and a hell of a lot about love. I'd learned how to kiss. How to sleep alongside someone. How stubble rash is not only painful, but also a 'dead giveaway'. How to count the hours until you see him. How to be too happy. How to forgive him when he cheats on you. How to let him back in. How to have to let him go. And I learned all that from one man.

I was heartbroken, lonely, and disillusioned.

Someone help me, help me,
help me please.

One early evening, I was alone, feeling particularly miserable, sitting in the living room of the house that I shared with three other students, watching the television and waiting for a music programme.

I had assumed the responsibility of making our own in-house *MTV*, never missing any of the Saturday morning kids shows, *Top Of The Pops* and *The Chart Show*, and recording anything and everything onto a composite video that would provide an opportunity not only to keep us up to date with what was happening musically, but also to save we poor pasta-eating students some money into the bargain.

There was a tape set in the machine, ready to roll if something caught my eye and ear.

Terry Wogan was introducing his nightly chat show, and he announced the guests who would be joining him that evening... *and singing his new single, Donny Osmond.*

I had not heard hide nor hair of Donny Osmond for about a decade. I had not played an Osmond record for years. except for maybe the opening track off that Christmas album to get me in the mood for the festive season.

Ah well, let's push the record button, for old times' sake.

The song was called *I'm In It For Love*. And it wasn't bad. It wasn't bad at all. Actually, it was quite good. Very good. In fact, I loved it.

He hadn't changed much. The face was the same. The hair was a long and softly curled mullet. When he cracked a smile, those pearly whites were still gleaming away. He answered the questions with a guarded maturity, and when he spoke of the past, he sounded slightly wistful, his memories tempered with an engaging humility. When Wogan asked if he regretted anything from his life, he said *Look, what kid wouldn't want to experience what I went through?*

And, as he talked, the women in the audience – now in their thirties, maybe married, maybe mothers – were still screaming and sighing at their teenage idol.

When Wogan picked up on this reaction and reminded Donny of his *Puppy Love* days, his response was both honest, poignant and generous. He admitted that it had held him back professionally in a business that does not readily accept change, or allow a child star to grow up, and that he had hated that song for a while, and all it that it represented.

But then, as he acknowledged, it had been such an important moment not only in his life, but in the lives of his fans, and to damn the song was to deny them their memories.

And I realised that I was now old enough to have some memories.

Everything we experience contributes to the person we become, for better or for worse, and we should never be ashamed of our past, because it has brought us to the present.

I went out the next day and bought the 12-inch single of *I'm In It For Love*, and I played it to death. I dug out and dusted off my old Osmond records, and made a compilation cassette of my favourite songs, which now had an entirely new meaning for me.

There were certainly some smiles of nostalgia for the more well-known tracks, those singles that reminded me of listening to Radio Luxembourg under the blankets after lights out, that I had willed up the charts and noted with pride in my notebooks.

There were songs that reminded me of those hours, days, months spent locked away in my bedroom, wearing out the needle of my record player as I pored over my collection of magazines and books.

And there were songs that now had a particular and peculiar resonance to my current state of rejection by the man I loved, as I walked around the lake beside my college, tearfully resigned to the fact that there would never be *A Time for Us*.

Maybe, if I'd thrown myself in, my old swimming teacher would have been there to save me.

I wonder what happened to him?

Any dream will do

We all need something to call our own, no matter how peculiar others may find it. It's fun to find something that the rest of the world doesn't fully comprehend, and may greet with snide derision, and, let's face it, if we all liked the same things, what a dull world the place would be.

While it is fun to self-indulge ourselves in what is now lamely termed our *guilty pleasure*, sometimes we need to gather with others who share our particular peculiarities, to share our best kept secret and maybe to feel like we are not the only odd one out.

The very-importantly-titled Donny Osmond International Network, with whom I forged a link after another chance sighting on the back of an album sleeve, announced the date for a fan club get-together.

It was just too camp to resist.

I had never been to any kind of convention before, but I had seen pictures of Trekkies and *Star Wars* fans, all done up to the nines and brandishing their light sabres.

But what would one wear to an Osmond convention? My treasured red velvet Donny cap, purchased when I was nine, wouldn't cover half my head and – gay as I may be – I'm not wearing a rosette for anybody's money. But an effort to dress for the occasion should and must be made.

My local newsagents offered a T-shirt printing service which offered the perfect solution. I bought a second-hand copy of *The Plan* album from a vendor in Greenwich Market, cut out the group picture on the cover, photocopied my old fan club badge, which I still had (and have), and had the pictures burned onto a white polo shirt.

Thus, dressed to impress, I was on my way to Wem-ber-ley!!!

As I walked into the room, I scanned the already healthy number of women, all avidly poring over the welcoming stalls of merchandise and memorabilia. All of a certain age, all casually dressed, and all slightly shyly looking at each other, as if they'd had to pluck up the courage to attend this meeting of Osmond Fans Anonymous.

It is one thing to sit in your living room, in your slacks and slippers, eating cold rice pudding out of the tin and singing away to your scratchy copy of *Alone Together*, but quite another to enter a room and meet others who very possibly do exactly the same.

It was slightly reminiscent of the *Stepford Wives*, if the *Stepford Wives* bought their clothes in *Evans* and weren't strangers to a home-perm.

There have been other times in my life when I was more than aware that I was in the minority, and not because I am gay, but because I am a man.

One was a Barry Manilow concert, and another was a k.d lang concert. You can actually see the tumbleweed blowing around the gentleman's toilets on those evenings.

There was not another man in the place and I swiftly became an object of whispered interest. Was I a security guard? Was I some long-suffering husband who had been dragged along as the designated driver? Or was I someone who had been strolling along the corridors, found out what was going on and had just bust into the room to take the piss?

Some of the conventionalists were looking at me as if I had walked into a steam room on a *women only* day, and kept eyeing me with a nervous suspicion. There was an almost audible sigh of relief when I removed my jacket to reveal my polo shirt, emblazoned with those five smiling faces.

It's alright, girls, he's one of us. And where did he get that shirt??

Two of the organisers came over and introduced themselves. Carolyn and Maggie, jolly Northerners both, and clearly up for a giggle. Once we had established that I was a genuine fan, we relaxed and chatted away, acknowledging both how special and how silly this day could and should be, and how we were going to do our damnedest to make it a little bit of both.

As we strolled around the stands covered with pictures, badges, scarves, and records, some of which I didn't know existed, I quickly got used to being told that meeting a male Osmond fan was as rare as finding that infamous hen's tooth. As we chatted, I couldn't help but like these women, who had run away from their families for a few hours to remember a more innocent time and to revisit their youth.

There was a big screen, showing films from the Seventies that I knew, and stuff from the Eighties that I didn't. I felt almost ashamed that I had taken a decade-long sabbatical, whereas a lot of these women had remained fiercely loyal. Some sat, gazing at the screen, silently mouthing along with the words, or giggling and nudging their neighbour if their particular favourite Osmond was strutting his stuff on the stage. I became quickly aware that some of these women had known each other for years, and that this wasn't just a convention, this was a reunion of old and true friends.

I'd walked into a family reunion.

The air was filled with shrieks of laughter, that particular sound you hear when a group of women get together, without the dampener of some damn man to dull the fun.

By the end of the day, I found myself adopted by a gang of women who were clearly up for a laugh, and we labelled ourselves *the naughty girls*, after the ones who used sit on the back row of the bus, passing loud comments on the other passengers and writing obscene messages in the condensation to torture the driver in the van behind.

We all openly acknowledged that, although we were all *bona fide* Osmond fans, today was all about having a giggle with like-minded souls, singing along with the songs we loved and escaping from our everyday lives, and turning back the clock to that age of innocence, and falling happily backwards into our first, last, and forever puppy love.

I was one of the boys who's one of the girls, and happy to be so.

But wait! Hold the front page! Big news!!

Sir Andrew Lloyd Webber announced that he was going to celebrate his 50th birthday in style at the Royal Albert Hall.

Among the impressive roster of guests, singing two songs from his successful appearance as Joseph in the *Technicolour Dreamcoat* show…Donny Osmond.

There was no power on God's good earth, no wind, no rain, no winters cold, no mountain high enough nor valley low enough that was going to stop me from seeing this show.

At 8am I was sat on the steps outside the Hall, waiting for the box office to open, just like those girls outside the Rainbow in 1972. The ticket price of £85 was the highest I had ever paid for a night of anything, but – two hours later – I held that precious piece of paper in my hand.

I was going to see Donny Osmond.

As if this wasn't exciting enough, I made my now daily call to a fan club phone line, and heard the recorded message that Donny was going to combine his visit to London with a *get-together* at a London hotel. He would answer questions, sing some songs, and then... *gasp*... meet and have a photograph taken with every attendee.

I duly submitted my name, and my place was confirmed.

Not only was I going to see Donny Osmond...

I was going to *meet* Donny Osmond.

This is the moment

What do you wear to meet your idol?

Definitely not the velvet cap, not the polo shirt, and *never* the rosette. I plumped for something formal. A black velvet jacket, blue velvet waistcoat, crisp white shirt tie, black trousers and boots. If this moment was going to be captured in a photograph, I wanted to look as presentable as possible. No spots, thank God, haircut looking good, teeth up to Osmond standard.

Good to go, and ready for my close-up.

As I sat on the train, heading into town, my heart was pounding. This was ridiculous! The whole situation was ridiculous! But fabulously ridiculous. What am I going to do when I meet him? What am I going to say? What is *he* going to do and say to me? This is madness!

I arrived at the hotel that would house the meeting. I was stupidly early, and wandered aimlessly around the streets as London awoke and started to hum with the sound of traffic. I had all these songs careering round my mind, a collage of pictures, snatches of videos, a kaleidoscope of memories that had been collected over a quarter of a century, and all connected to a man I was just about to meet.

Cometh the hour, cometh the man.

As I entered the hotel, the foyer was full of women, many of whom I recognised from the convention, and all of whom were done in up their best outfits. I sat on a sofa with a small group of pals, and admitted that I was stupidly over-excited.

One of them put her arm around me, and asked – in a voice not dissimilar to a nurse wheeling a patient towards the operating theatre – *Is this your first time?* It had been a long time since anyone had asked me that, but, in this case, it was absolutely true.

Most of them had already met Donny, and were sharing stories and comparing notes, just as soldiers share old war tales and compare medals. Everyone assured me that Donny was *really lovely*, and they seemed to get a certain thrill out of seeing someone about to experience what they had been through many times.

I felt like the last virgin behind the bike sheds.

The doors opened to the room and we entered, in strictly numbered order. Whoever had left their name first on the phone line got a seat nearer to the front. I found myself in the third row, once again the only man in the entire room, and looking at a small empty stage with an upright piano, as the buzz of excited conversation rose and anticipation filled the room. It wasn't the Rainbow, it wasn't Earls Court…but any minute now…

Julie, the network creator, stood in front of the stage, and said, softly and simply *Ladies and gentleman…*(that was just for me!)…*Donny Osmond.*

And there he was.

Black leather jacket, black roll-neck jumper, black trousers, black shoes, suspiciously *dark to the roots* brown hair… *Donny bloody Osmond.*

An instant standing ovation, cheering, applause… and no screaming!

He took a microphone and started to speak. He spoke about why he had been away from England for so long, about being in Joseph, about his family, about taking classes in church, about the Donny and Marie show, about anything and everything that anyone asked and wanted to know. He answered each question in a serious and considered way, but was never too far away from finding humour in both the past and the present. He clearly knew a lot of the women in the audience, and smiled warmly at them, as if greeting an old friend.

I had submitted a question asking about how he had met Andrew Lloyd Webber. As he read out my name, he struggled with the pronunciation of my surname, and scoured the audience to find me.

I'm over here, Donny, the one without the breasts!

He looked me straight in the eye, and told the tale about how he auditioned in front of the Dark Lord himself for the role Joseph, and was told right there and then that he had got the job.

I was a total stranger to him and he answered my question as he would to a journalist. Directly, seriously, without fluff or flannel.

I later found out that he thought I *was* a journalist. He just assumed that any man in the room was there for professional reasons. Having been on the end of so much derision from men for almost all of his professional life, he was understandably wary. He would also admit that it took a considerable length of time to get over the fear that every man in every audience was only there to ridicule and run him down.

There was a moment that made my heart stop, and for all the wrong reasons. Without reason or warning, he suddenly adopted this very prissy sibilant voice, while talking about

47

embracing his *feminine side.* He then quipped, almost off microphone, *Yeah, me and Ellen, we're coming out. Yeah, right.*

I thought *Oh no. Please no. Please don't be a homophobic prat.*

I was aware that my kind of love was deemed to be a sin within the Mormon faith, with the usual proviso of *you can be it, you just can't do anything about it.* But, with all those years in show business, the one profession where *my people* might just be in the majority, surely, Sir, you cannot have a problem.

I let it go, and it was forgotten as quickly as it had been said.

After over an hour of Q&A, Donny announced a break before the second half of the event, which would include a quiz and some songs. So, 98% of the room head towards the ladies rest room, while 2% head to the gentleman's…

Two converging staircases led down to the basement, where the restroom was to be found, and – just like in a Hollywood musical – I found myself walking downstairs, step by step, opposite Donny Osmond.

I don't care how great a fan you are, *no-one* wants to meet their childhood hero while standing next to them at a urinal. What would you say? *Loved your last album.* Good grief, no.

I turned on a dime and headed back up the stairs. I could hold it.

As I mingled with some of the women in the foyer, they were all fascinated with *what it was like for me,* and I was delighted to share my absolute thrill of seeing Donny Osmond in the flesh. But when I shared the story that I could have seen a bit more flesh that any of them would *ever* get the chance to see, they were beside themselves.

Why didn't you go in? they wailed.
I would have done! said one.
Me too! said another.

As much and as clearly as I explained my decision, I was made to feel like I had missed a truly golden moment over the *Armitage Shanks*.

I'll never make a cottage queen.

Back to the day, and it was time for the individual *meet and greet* and the promised picture with the man himself. Once again, we were lined up, all ready to file in and be photographed. The hand mirrors were out, fresh mascara and lipstick was being applied, hair was being brushed...

And that was just me.

One by one, in they went. As I stood in the doorway, waiting my turn, I saw the set up within the room.

A small, two-seater sofa, with mercifully kind lighting.

As the camera snapped, Donny put his arm around the clearly delighted woman on the sofa next to him, and flashed that smile that had adorned every corner of my bedroom wall.

And now, this was my moment.

I walked into the room and said hello. He held out his hand and shook mine. I remarked how strange it was for both of us to be the only men in the room, and possibly how odd it must be for him to meet a genuine long-term male fan. He acknowledged that I was indeed in a very small club, but that he was nonetheless grateful to anyone who had supported him for so many years, regardless of gender.

Time to take the picture. We both knew the drill. Eyes to camera, smile, don't blink, and hold it. It was over in a literal flash. And his arm stayed firmly lowered behind the sofa, and not wrapped around my shoulder.

After the photo shoot and an overlong lyric quiz, it was into the final furlong and time for some songs. Some new, some old, and the one song that everyone really wanted to hear. As he sang *Puppy Love*, gently, almost soulfully, hitting every note on the nail, I silently wished everyone else in the room away.

I was back in my bedroom, my secret world, listening and learning about music, about lyrics, about chord structures, about arrangements, key changes, backing vocal. And I was learning about love. I was learning from the man now sitting barely fifteen feet away from me.

Where did all the good times go? They were right here, right now.

The past leads to the present and the present is a wonderful place to be.

The Birthday Concert was a two-hour celebration of musical theatre, and the work of its most successful composer. All the hits were there, from *Jesus Christ Superstar* and *Cats*, through to *Evita* and the all conquering *Phantom of the Opera*.

Glenn Close got the first standing ovation of the night with a superb rendition of *With One Look*, and Elaine Paige made sure that she remained the sole owner of *Memory* with a roof-raising performance of Lloyd Webber's most famous song.

Donny acquitted himself admirably with *Any Dream Will Do*, bar a little slip on the words, and was note perfect on *Close Every Door*. He was warmly welcomed onto the stage and generously applauded as he left.

Our man done good.

Caught up in the excitement at the end of the evening, I accepted the offer of a ride back to the St James Hotel, where the driver and every other self-respecting Osmond fan knew that Donny was staying. These women knew everything, from what time he had to be at the Hall for rehearsals, to what room he was staying in and probably what he had for breakfast.

Everything.

After a short wait, a large car pulled up and out stepped Donny, who was immediately swept up by the loving crowd that had gathered outside the hotel. He was clearly thrilled and relieved that the evening had gone so well. He was happy to pose for pictures and accept the numerous bunches of flowers.

As he stood on the steps of the hotel, fielding off questions and shouts of appreciation, one woman beside me shouted out *Donny, can I get a picture of you with Ian?* Apparently she was not alone as others called out the same request. I felt a little bit famous!

Donny called out *Ian, get up here!*

I duly accepted the invitation and stood alongside him on the steps of the St James Hotel. while a battery of cameras captured the moment. Donny got the devil in him, and teasingly said to the crowd *Hey, shall I kiss him?*

He followed this with a quick flex of his shoulders and a gruff *Yeah, how about them Bears?* in a comic imitation of the beer-swilling, football-watching, all-American male, who would rather throw himself under a herd of buffalo than be suspected of being attracted to another man.

I smiled.

He knew what he was doing. He knew who I was, what I was and what I could handle, and there was not one slither of malice or cruelty in what he said. We were doing what he knew we Brits love to do. Having a laugh.

It was time for one tired teenage idol to go to bed. We shook hands one more time, he waved to the fans and went through the doors of the hotel.

As I rejoined the crowd on the pavement, everyone was enthusing about how fabulous Donny had been that evening, and how the reviews had to be good enough to encourage more visits, more performances, maybe even a tour.

But even more than enthusiastic, they were proud. Proud of their idol, as if his performance had justified all those years of putting up with the playground ridicule, all that time and money spent, and all the faith and belief in the choice that they had made when they put that first picture on their wall.

I floated home on cloud nine.

As I quietly opened the bedroom door, the tall, dark and handsome man I lived with and loved so much took a sleepy-eyed look at me, smiled, and whispered *You're glowing.*

I put my arms around his neck and nestled my face into his chest. I felt his fur against my cheek, and his muscled arm around me. He let me stay there... and I thought *I am very happy here.*

> *I'll love you 'til the bluebells forget to bloom*
> *I'll love you 'til the clover has lost its perfume*
> *I'll love you 'til the poets run out of rhyme*
> *Until the Twelfth of Never*
> *And that's a long long time.*

We can be heroes

The day I met
David Bowie

There's a Starman, waiting in the sky

My first encounter with a hero was with my ultimate star-man, Mr David Bowie.

I cannot claim to have been one of those watching *Top Of The Pops* on July 6, 1972, who saw a skinny man in a quilted jumpsuit with a a shock of bright red hair slink his arm sexily round the neck of his guitarist and send shockwaves through living rooms across the country.

The first song I heard was the cavernous thump of *John, I'm Only Dancing*, a song for which the BBC had created a video using bikers riding around Battersea Power Station, though what this had to do with the very gay content of the song, heaven only knows.

I also have an embarrassing recollection of attending a garden party in 1972, and finding myself in charge of the record player, while my contemporaries splashed about in the swimming pool, or chased each other round the house, in a desperate search for their first feel and fumble. I spent far too long dancing with myself – or rather my spot-lit reflection in the patio windows – as some singer sang about floating round a tin can, far above the world.

And then there was an early evening documentary, voiced by some faceless and supercilious presenter, sneeringly describing Bowie's cosmetic transformation into his stage persona, which by this time was the glamorously gaudy Aladdin Sane. As I watched in a mix of fascination and awe, I wondered what I would look like with no eyebrows, rouged cheeks and a gold circle on my forehead.

Well, I had some wax crayons, and I knew where Dad kept his razor, and the house was empty…

And...*I looked fabulous!*
Then I looked at the clock.

Not so much Aladdin Sane but a lad in trouble.

She who would beat my bottom was due home at any minute. I desperately tried to remove the wax crayon from my face, scrubbing my skin raw with a flannel, with only a modicum of success. The shaven eyebrows were another matter entirely. My mother was utterly unamused by the sight of her youngest son, and I was sent to school the next day with my fringe glued over my forehead, in a feeble attempt to hide my handiwork.

My lifelong love affair with Bowie began in earnest in the late Seventies. I started safely enough with a greatest hits collection, before backtracking to the glory days of Ziggy Stardust and working onwards and upwards. It was a fascinating and at times challenging journey. Each new album was a radical departure from its predecessor, and just when I had grown accustomed to one face and one style, and perfected my take on the slicked back hair and the sunken cheekbones, it was time to get off the *Soul Train* and board the *Transeurope Express* to the depths of Berlin.

I worked damn hard to wrap my head round the doom and gloom of *Low*, and had just about got there when *Heroes* was released. I remember sitting in my room, trying to make sense of what I was hearing, before having to admit defeat and declare that I just couldn't go with him on this one. Abroad on a family holiday in Crete, however, all I could think about what was this album and, on my return home, I raced upstairs to put needle to vinyl and surrender to what remains to this day as one of my favourite pieces from his extensive catalogue of extraordinary work.

I was blessed beyond belief to be in New York City in 1981, at the same time as Bowie was performing as John Merrick in *The Elephant Man* at the Booth Theatre. My beloved high school art teacher secured me a front row seat for a Saturday matinee, and my heart was leaping out of my mouth as the lights dimmed and the show began.

After a short opening scene, the stage was plunged into darkness, and then a single spotlight from above shone down on the loin-clothed figure of David Bowie.

As a narrator described the appalling physical deformities of this tragic man, Bowie curled and crumpled his body into a contorted, limp, and pathetic aberration of the human form.

When he spoke, his voice was transformed into a strangled hiccup, and that face that had stared so proudly and defiantly from under a mask of make up was now exposed, naked and vulnerable.

It was a truly extraordinary performance, and when he walked on at the end for his bow, miraculously upright after two hours bent out of shape, the audience bellowed their approval, and I clapped my hands together until they burned.

I never thought that I would get so close to my hero again.

But I did.

1986, and I found myself on the set of *Absolute Beginners*, a lush pop video extended into a film by Julien Temple. The cast was a surreal collective of undiscovered and established stars, including a very young Patsy Kensit, who was still as sweet as the moment when the moment when the pod went pop, the veteran comic Eric Sykes, the DJ Alan Freeman and the very ebullient Lionel Blair, who kept on touching my tummy.

Bowie was cast as the cold and calculating advertising executive, Vendice Partners, and was dressed in a crisp blue suit and tie, with his hair brushed back in a 1950s pompadour.

You always knew when he was coming onto the set or into a room. There was this very particular rush of excitement, heads would turn and necks would stretch, whispers would fly from mouth to ear, and then he would appear, haloed in his own aura and charisma, walking slowly, effortlessly elegant, graciously aloof but always disarmingly charming.

Of course, there is an unwritten rule that you never *ever* ask the star for a photo. It just isn't the done thing, and may well result in being thrown off the set. Added to this, his faithful assistant and personal Rotweiller, Coco Scwhab, never left his side, except for when he was filming.

This was going to take all kinds of guts.

Actually, it took no guts at all. He just happened to come out of his trailer, walked over and I asked him. And, like the perfect gentleman he was, he agreed and stood beside me while the camera clicked and captured the moment.

The picture adorns my study wall to this day.

With my hair held aloft by a winning combination of teasing and hairspray, I am grinning away like the cat that bought shares in cream, and my all-time hero standing beside me, besuited and beautiful, hands on hips, and smiling, safe in the knowledge that he was more than making my day. It looks for all the world like me and my mate Dave, and what we did on our holidays.

Wherever I have lived, that picture is on my wall.

Something happened on the day he died...

January 10 2016
6.50 am.

I am propped up in the bed, cradling my laptop, watching the video of *Sue (In a Season of Crime),* the original version of a song featured on the brilliant new album *Blackstar,* which had been released two days previously, and had been on repeated play all weekend.

My phone vibrates. It's a text from my mate Paul.

It reads *Don't worry. It's a hoax.*

I tap back *What's a hoax?*

A moment of cyber silence.

He replies *Oh shit. It's not a hoax.*

I'm irritated but not yet overly concerned as I text *WHAT?*

Two words. *Bowie's died.*

Time, no longer waiting in the wings, stands still and centre stage. I'm out of bed, downstairs, still clutching my phone, turning on the television, and kneeling, naked and shivering with cold and dread, in front of the screen.

It's business as normal at the BBC.

The 7am news begins. Nothing.

I text back. *Nothing on the news. Hoax.*

The reply comes with a picture of a screen.

Sky News. Bowie's face. And the word *Dead.*

And within that second... *We have breaking news...*

Heavy breaths. Shuddering. Gasping.

And then...here come the tears.

I watch and sob as the tribute plays out, repeatedly saying to myself, but out loud, *no…no…no.*

As the newsreader concludes the item with the words *David Bowie, who died this morning,* I wail like an animal.

At 7.20, the first phone call from a friend comes through, gently checking that I have heard the news. I cannot speak. Just sob. I apologise for being so silly. And sob even harder.

After over an hour of watching every news broadcast and hearing the same safe selection of sounds and visions, I feel the need to choose my own hymn to wing my hero on his way.

Grabbing my iPod, I scroll down the 800 plus songs in my collection, with no real idea of what to play. Fast or slow? Seventies? Eighties? *Tin Machine?* No, not *Tin Machine.* A classic? What?

For no reason whatsoever, I select *The Wide-Eyed Boy From Freecloud*, a lesser-known album track from his second solo album, not performed on stage since the now legendary rock'n'roll suicide of Ziggy Stardust at the Hammersmith Odeon in 1973.

The song tells the tale of a mystical young man, imprisoned and facing the death sentence. Or, as Bowie himself says

It was about the disassociated, the ones who feel as though they're left outside, which was how I felt about me. I always felt I was on the edge of events, the fringe of things, and left out.

Amen to that.

As the guitars strummed, as the orchestral strings swelled, and as that voice – that unique voice which had spoken and sung to me for over forty years – told the story of a young man, forced to pay with his life for the crime of being different, I started to move, to dance…

And I saw my own reflection in the glass of the french windows of my dining room that separated and protected me from the dark cold dawn of this dreadful day, and I saw and remembered that little boy, dancing with himself at a suburban garden party to the strange and seductive strains of *Space Oddity*.

And I let him go, as my hero sang to me and rose up to the heavens…

You'll lose me, though I'm always really free

My hero. For ever and ever.

A straight talk
from a bent speaker

The day I met
Quentin Crisp

The happiest days of your life

I was born in Sutton in 1962, at the same hospital, I am proud to say, as Quentin Crisp.

The family home was in Kingswood in Surrey, right on the buckle of the commuter belt. It was a world of substantial and detached houses, immaculately trimmed lawns, tennis clubs and village halls, coffee mornings and dinner parties where everyone knew everyone, everyone sang from the same eminently respectable and rigidly conservative hymn sheet, and the most shocking sight would have been a woman shopping in the village wearing a pair of trousers.

Play your cards right, and you could complete your education, marry the girl down the lane, send your children away to boarding school as soon as they could stand, go to the city, *do well*, live, die and be buried in the local churchyard without ever having crossed the Brighton Road.

It was a very small and a very safe world.

I have some hazy black-and-white childhood memories, captured on the pages of the family photograph album, of sand pits and paddling pools, of arranged play dates with acceptable playmates, and of the annual August holidays in Devon and on the Isle of Wight.

But the pictures that make me smile the most are those of the weird and wonderful outfits I created from many happy hours of delving into the dressing up box, draping myself in fabrics far more exotic in my imagination than in reality.

My primary school years were only noteworthy for raps with a ruler round the back of the knees from my draconian headmistress when I failed to answer simple Maths questions, and the unbridled excitement when the Christmas lunch of a single sausage was accompanied by an inch of champagne, or *Tizer*, as it was more commonly known.

In 1975 – after five years at a local preparatory school where the Headmaster wore a kilt, where we answered the register in Latin, the school plays were drastically abridged works by Shakespeare, and swimming costumes were banned for the compulsory dips in the outdoor unheated pool – it was time to pack a trunk, slip into a new and ill-fitting uniform, and head down the motorway to Cheltenham.

I was 13 and small for my age, so small that my family nickname was Mouse. I had visited the College on several occasions, accompanying my family to the annual summer Speech Day, and to drop and collect my brother, who had been a student for the past two years. But this time was not a visit.

This time was to stay.

It began with a tea party.

Thirteen young men standing with their parents, unable to wrap their mouths around a sandwich let alone a sentence, eyeing each other suspiciously and knowing that any minute would be the moment of goodbye, and that there were to be no tears. Big boys don't cry.

When the matron announced, as kindly as she could, *Well, I think it's time to go and unpack*, my throat tightened and my eyes blinked back the forbidden waterworks as I said farewell. We were then led through a doorway, and up a worn stone stairway to our dormitory, a long grey corridor of a room on the fourth floor, housing about thirty metal-framed beds, separated by wooden partition walls.

The only furniture was a single wooden chair and a chest of drawers, quickly stuffed with the contents of your trunk, the regulation shirts, socks and pants, before the sportswear was decanted and transported down to a peg in the communal changing room, that still smelt of last summer's sweat.

We were then marched out for an audition for the choir. My brother had advised me to flunk the audition, as parading down the chapel aisle every Sunday – dressed like an angel in a white surplice – was not going to help the process of settling in. Despite the fact that I had been a concert soloist at my previous school I decided to hit enough flat and un-enthusiastic notes to avoid being chosen.

Finally, we were escorted to the Dining Hall, a former Chapel with stained glass windows and dark wood-panelled walls lined with portraits of demonic-looking headmasters, but now filled with long wooden tables with benches, where we queued up, grabbed a tray, collected our food from the servery, and wandered in search of a table that we could call our own. I felt like a prisoner, stripped bare, lost and confused, being inspected by these big, rough looking boys, all of whom checking the *fresh fish* for the slightest sign of weakness.

That evening, as I slid into a cold strange bed, the bed springs creaking, I heard the indecipherable murmurs of the other, older residents of the dormitory, a rumbling and uneasy lullaby to send me off into a sleepless night.

The house hand bell was rung at 7am, ending any chance of sleeping in. But just in case, another bell was rung ten min-utes later and the dormitory door was flung open, and a prefect marched down the aisle of the dormitory, barking the order to *rise and shine*, and stripping the bedclothes off the curled up bodies of any slug-a-beds.

After breakfast, we were summoned to a house meeting, where we were informed of a two-week *grace* period, where we would have neither cleaning tasks nor punishments, in order to allow us to settle into College life and learn the rules of the House.

At 8.30, the bell rang to herald the mass exodus to College and the daily early morning worship.

The Chapel was even more impressive than the Dining Hall. A majestic pipe organ looked down over the inward-facing pews that sandwiched the black-and-white tiled aisle which led the eye past the ornate pulpit to the altar, covered with a white cloth and crowned with an ornate gold cross, behind which was a facade of stone sculpture and stained glass.

I sat in the front row of the allocated pew, and gazed at all this splendour and at the sea of sullen faces. It was the first time I had seen the entire population of the school under one roof. *Christ, there's a lot of people.*

The organ drone was suddenly punctuated by the march of steel-heeled shoes, as the College Prefects marched down the aisle with military precision and that hard-jawed arrogance that comes from being a big fish in a small pool.

The opening bars of the hymn swelled and filled this vast space, the congregation rose as one and started to sing…

And it was all broken voices!

Coming from an all-boys school, I was used to hearing the hymn sung in that unmistakeable boy treble. Here, it was sung by men. Young men, but men nonetheless, with deeper voices, some with five o'clock shadows, others who had already gone through their growth spurt, and were tall, broad, muscular.

Not all, you understand, but from the perspective of a boy called Mouse, I felt like a Hobbit.

The following weeks were a rush of new teachers, new subjects, new rules and regulations. The schoolday lasted from 9am until 6pm, three days a week. On the other three, lessons ended at lunchtime, leaving the afternoon free for sports. In the evenings, there was silent study period between 7pm and 9pm, then a half hour hot chocolate break before bed, lights out and silence in the dormitory at 9.30.

You could only wear your own clothes on Saturday evening and on Sunday after the full Chapel Service, and you were not to leave the College premises without written permission from your housemaster, who also banked whatever parental allowance had been allocated to cover haircuts, tuck and half-term travel.

Not that it was at all regimented, you understand…

Let's start the descent into the inferno.
Public schools teach power structures.

In your first year, you are the scum of the earth and you must be treated as such.

Once the two-week *grace* period is over, you are responsible for your house cleaning duty: dusting, hoovering and washing down the communal areas, including the toilets. Your work will be inspected, and if the prefect's finger picks up some dust, you have to do it all over again.

And there was fagging.

The practice of a senior student 'owning' a younger boy as a personal slave, expected to make the master's toast, shine his shoes, clean his study, make his tea and, in extreme cases, warm his toilet seat and his bed, had supposedly been stopped in the year I arrived, but the new prefects were reluctant to let it go.

Some shady deals were struck, and sometimes financial reward was offered for the previously mentioned services. No-one saw anything wrong in it. The master got shiny shoes and the fag got a shiny coin to spend in the tuck shop. It was business as usual, the old school tradition maintained.

In the basement of the house was a small television room, with nowhere near enough seats for the seventy residents. Anyone in a lower year could be asked to surrender their seat to a senior, via the grotesquely titled practice of *jewing out* which resulted in the front row being dominated by the taller boys, while the younger and smaller ones sat behind, searching for a sightline over heads or between shoulders.

There was not one minute of the day when you were alone. No place for privacy. No escape. Nowhere to hide.

At the age of thirteen, everything is in flux, and everyone is looking to make sure that they are exactly the same as everyone else. Your body is changing by the minute, and change is frightening at the best of times. And the only thing more frightening than a changing body is one that seems to be taking its time to catch up. Boys check each other out, whether they admit it or not. They might not want to touch each other, but a sneaky peek in the changing room doesn't mean that you are a big homo. You're just…checking.

I was checking. Oh boy, was I checking.

But, checking out another man whilst naked and in a public space could lead to a very embarrassing situation, signing and sealing your fate for eternity. Added to this was my absolute mortification at the lack of any decent sign of puberty, and so the changing rooms and communal showers became the site of huge anxiety. I started to find any excuse to avoid sport and having to change and shower with the other boys, which was instantly noted and became a source of interrogation and humiliation.

My appendix saved me. It ruptured three weeks after arriving at College, and I found myself in hospital, having the damn thing taken out. I was sent home to recuperate for three weeks, with the date of my return to College set for the start of the next half of term.

By the time I returned, my fate was sealed.

All the gang-forming that occurs when a group of young people get together was done, dusted and set in stone, and I was in a gang of one.

Due to the enforced period of recuperation, I was mercifully still unable to participate in sporting activities, which saved me from being trampled into the mud of the rugby field, not only by the opposing team but my own. While this saved me from fear of exposure in the showers, it branded me as weak and pathetic, an unworthy member of the house. This, is turn, led to the traditional abuse being flung in my direction.

I was a fairy. I was a poof. I was a queer.

To enclose a load of young bucks from morning until night in a confined space is a recipe for disaster. Boys fight, even with their friends. The impulse to poke, punch, grab and wrestle is fuelled by the need to flex some muscle and to show who is king of the forest. Fear and intimidation were the order of the day, and if you were sensible, you swore your allegiance to the *king* and did his bidding. If you wanted to survive, you had to run with the pack and be seen to be loyal, obedient and *one of the lads*.

In the dormitory, there were three *kings*, all strapping lads who ruled the sweat room with a bullish swagger. During the day, I did my utmost to stay out of their way, but after lights out, there was no escape.

Their favourite trick was to ask someone in a higher year group to come into the dormitory as the lights were about to be turned out, and tell me that the Housemaster wanted to see me, a command not to be ignored, and which saw me wrapped in my dressing gown, descending the stairs and knocking on his study door.

Of course, he didn't want to see me, and I was sternly ordered back to bed. As I entered the darkened dormitory, I was greeted by the stinging lash of wet towels, and ran the gauntlet of pain that whipped me back to my bed.

Every boy was allocated a daily small bottle of milk, but there was no fridge to keep milk cold, so that in the summertime, the contents turned to yogurt before anyone returned to the house. But all the bottles had to be emptied and cleaned out and left for collection the next day. Or –alternatively – smashed up and placed in my bed, creating a studded sheet of broken glass that embedded into my skin.

On one particularly terrifying night, after the usual pushing, punching and strangling, two of the three *kings* grabbed me and pushed me towards the window at the end of my cubicle. The remaining one threw it open, and they tipped me up and over, each grabbing an ankle, before feeding me head-first out of the window, so that I was hanging outside, four flights up, and looking down at a concrete yard below and – if they dropped me – certain death.

I didn't scream. I was too scared to scream. Scared that if I screamed they would let me fall. After seconds that felt like minutes, I was hauled back and left shaking and sobbing on the floor, as my tormentors smirked and strutted back their beds, to a round of congratulatory applause.

I had never felt so alone in my life.

You may ask *Why didn't you tell someone?*

I did. I told my parents. I got down on my hands and knees and begged them to take me away from this hellish existence. The answer was *No.* I had got into a highly respected school, the fees were paid, the family legacy must be continued, and I had to stick it out. When I heard that nonsensical sentence *It will make a man of you*, I knew that my plea had fallen on deaf ears.

So…alone. Absolutely alone.

The love that dare not speak its name

There is a school of thought, fed by myths and movies, that the young men privileged enough to have enjoyed the joys of private education spent most of their schooldays putting their privates not only on parade but into each other.

From the whisky-soaked bore in *Four Weddings and a Funeral*, with his misty-arsed remembrance of the boy who *buggered him senseless*, to Lord Grantham musing how sore his fist would have been if he had punched *every boy at Eton who tried to kiss him*, it was considered an acceptable adolescent rite of passage, if you pardon the pun.

Whilst not condoned, it was deemed that any furtive fondlings would be ejaculated out of the system and would not interfere with the plan to marry a girl in the next county, who would happily make the breakfast, the beds and the babies.

But this cock-ettish behaviour was only acceptable amongst the most senior boys in the school, in another peacock display of their power and untouchable arrogance, and whether it was anything more than a public flirtation without any private fulfilment, I cannot say.

There were the inevitable rumours about boys who were *bum chums*, but as nothing was ever seen, nothing was ever said, and certainly no-one was ever confronted. It was excused as an expression of the *special relationship* that exists between men, and more to do with the connection of souls rather than the sordid act of making the beast with two backs.

One early evening, doing the mail collection, I knocked on the door of a prefect's private study, and was told to enter. As I opened the door, it was sharply kicked shut from inside. I knocked again, and this time the door opened. The Head of House was recumbent on a cushion-covered mattress that served as a sofa, with his shirt unbuttoned to the navel. Very Rupert Everett. Lying beside him was a prefect, in a similar state of…relaxation.

The Head told me to come in. The door was closed behind me. He told me that he knew that I was finding it hard settling-in, and that he was aware that I was being bullied in a *particular* way. As he offered words of support and a friendly ear if it *all got too much*, the prefect beside him snuggled in, placing a leg over his groin and gently stroking his chest, both of them looking intently at me and for my reaction to this display of homoerotic intimacy.

I was speechless, stunned and scared. I had never seen two men being so sensual with each other. *What am I supposed to do?* Join in? Absolutely not. *Are they being serious?* Or is this a ruse to get me to admit something which will be spread it round the house to confirm suspicion and justify my daily beatings?

Either which way, I said nothing. I collected the mail, closed the door, and moved on and away.

In the film *If*, directed by Lindsay Anderson, himself an old Cheltonian who had somehow managed to get his anarchic damnation of the public school system filmed on the very site of his personal Hades, there is an incredibly beautiful and erotic scene where a younger boy watches a senior, flying in slow motion on the parallel bars in a gymnasium.

It is the most powerful portrayal of the awakening of love that I have ever seen. There is no physical contact between the boys, and only the merest hint of an exchanged smile. But it is the look of wonder on the younger boy's face, as he watches the object of his burgeoning desire, that captures the moment of realisation and the dream of that forbidden love.

I found my love on a rugby field.

He had golden wavy hair like Apollo, blue eyes that blazed like a panther, and thighs that could crack walnuts. He was short, stocky, and wore the tiniest shorts I had ever seen. Not only was he breathtakingly handsome, but rumour had it he was hung like a horse, and used the bass bin of his speakers as a vibrator. I have no idea about whether the last two details are true, but I have never been able to listen to *Whole Lotta Love* by Led Zeppelin, with that insistent and thundering baseline, without imagining this Adonis discovering his own particular musical nirvana.

Few things could have encouraged me to waste my Saturday afternoon standing in the wind and rain on a muddy touchline watching the College XV fight it out against another team of likely lads, but for him, it was worth it. He was fast and fearless, and a vision in striped shirt, socks and sweat. I used to gasp if ever he was brutally tackled, and wanted to beat his assailant into the ground, as if I even had the strength to throw the ball back should it bounce my way.

When he became a College prefect, I would live for the moment every morning when he would wait outside the door to enter the Chapel, and I would watch him from my carefully selected seat, convincing myself that he was smiling at me, and dream my dirty little dreams as I watched him walk down the aisle. I would feel a thrill if I saw him walk through the Quad, his few books tucked underneath his muscular arm, as I struggled along with my overstuffed briefcase.

I used to fantasise about walking through the Dining Hall with my tray, pretending to look for somewhere to sit and eat, and him gesturing for me to join him.

In the summer months, when the uniform was reduced to *shirt sleeve order*, I would look at him lying on the grass, watching the cricket, with his shirt open, and wish that I was a bead of sweat, trickling down his chest…

We never spoke to one another. Not one word.

But my eyes adored him.

Two and a half years of teenage torture passed and the beatings grew fewer as I got bigger and more senior, but the abuse and exclusion by the majority remained intact.

I found a few friends within my year group, drawn to my sense of humour and my ability to imitate the members of staff, and I was one of the first kids on the block to get into punk, which gave me certain kudos.

But I was still wearing the label that others had pinned on me when I was not only a homosexual virgin, but I looked the same as everyone else.

Something had to happen. Something had to change.

In Spring 1978, I was watching the television when a trailer was run for a programme to be shown later that evening. As the song *The Sun Has Got His Hat On* played, the screen showed a hand with bright red painted fingernails. The camera panned up to reveal hair of similar hue, flowing out from under a wide-brimmed black hat, framing a face plastered with powder, mascara and lipstick…and the person wearing all this paraphernalia was a man.

The film was *The Naked Civil Servant*, and the man was John Hurt, playing the part of a man of whom I had never heard…

Quentin Crisp.

I *had* to see this film.

Fortunately, my parents rarely stayed up after the *9 o'clock News* had finished, and thus when the programme began, I was alone.

From the opening image of a four-year-old boy, bedecked in his mother's dress and jewels, dancing in front of a mirror, I was entranced. It was my one-boy presentation of *The Sound of Music*, aged six, which climaxed with a white pillowcase wedding veil and a bouquet of coloured pencils. It was Bowie and the wax crayons and the shaved eyebrows. It was...me.

When he declared that his homosexuality should not be kept as a hidden and shameful secret, but must displayed for all the world the world to see, I was inspired, watching in drop-jawed admiration at his flagrant exhibitionism, and applauding the shockwaves of horror his appearance caused amongst the wartime Londoners as he paraded the streets of Pimlico, *dumb with lipstick and blinded by mascara*.

It was a call to arms.

On my return to College, I plucked up sufficient courage to place an order for a copy of *The Naked Civil Servant* in the school bookshop, and was relieved that the lady in charge seemed none the wiser and neither censored nor reported my purchase. Within a week, the book had arrived. I read and absorbed every last word on every page, learning about his situation, his journey, his choices, his decisions, his wit, his wisdom, and his ultimate guide to survival.

And if he could do it, I could too.

What was I learning from Quentin Crisp?

Quite simply, that the most effective weapon you have is all and everything you are.

Once you acknowledge what others consider your weakness, you can set about turning it into your greatest strength. When you take all that others want to ridicule, and feed it, nurture it and wear it as a medal of honour, you are untouchable.

I learned that the most effective way to avoid being victimised was not to retaliate with a punch, a kick or a mouthful of anger, but to present my tormentors with their worst nightmare.

In other words, if you want a queer, you're going to get the biggest queer in the world, the like of which you never even dared to dream.

It took a few weeks to gather the nerve to prepare for what I knew I had to do, and I cannot remember the breaking point, if indeed there was one.

But whenever it was, it was time.

I sneaked into town, went to Boots, and dredged up the courage to approach the counter and buy foundation powder, mascara, eyeliner, eyeshadow and blusher. I decided against lipstick. I didn't want to shock them, after all.

I also bought some blonde hair dye. Blondes have more fun, apparently.

By this stage of my school career, I had my own study bedsit, with a pin board wall covered with pictures of David Bowie, Marc Bolan and the group Japan, all of them no strangers to a little bit of cosmetic enhancement. I stared at them, looking for clues. How do I do this? *Can* I do this?

I waited until after 10pm, when I was certain I would not be disturbed and discovered.

I crept down the darkened stairwell to the showers, wet my head under the water and applied the hair colouring, feeling the heat as it burned away the brown, leaving me – twenty minutes later – with a sandy blonde. Not quite as white as I wanted, but it would do for starters.

Back in my study, I opened up my bag of treasures. I was a reasonable artist and was used to painting with brushes and sponges. But now the canvas was my face. I began with a basecoat of foundation, an initially tentative then a bolder stroke of mascara, a tracing of eyeliner, and some experimental work with the palette of eyeshadow.

Time to reflect on my reflection…and there I was.

Or at least, a version of myself. A tougher version.
Defiant. Queer.

Breakfast was skipped. I stayed in my room, undisturbed, and prepared myself. I'd got the hang of it now. All good to go. When I was sure that everyone was out of the house and on the way to the morning service, I headed out onto the street, in all my glorious glory.

People on their way to work stopped and stared. And stared. And stared. I didn't feel like they were staring at me, just the paintwork, my new suit of armour.

Whatever fear I felt – and my insides were revolving like a washing machine on final rinse and spin – was kept at bay by the fact that, at last, I knew *why* people were looking at me differently.

I *was* different. I had *made* myself different.

The last stragglers were going into Chapel as I rounded the corner. No turning back now.

I walked along the path, climbed the steps and entered.

Eyes widened. Jaws dropped. Scowls from the staff. Gasps. Giggles. Disbelief and disgust.

Yep, that'll do for starters.

At the end of the service, I was grabbed by my furious housemaster, and escorted by a prefect to the Headmaster.

He wasn't too bad, actually.

A bit of a rebel himself, he acknowledged that *We all have to express ourselves blah blah blah, the Beatles blah blah blah, individualism blah blah blah*, but rules were rules, and I was ordered to wash my face and return my hair to its original colour. I was marched to a local chemist, selected some brown hair dye, and was even supervised while applying it.

Ah, Sir, but brown on top of blonde makes red. Ziggy Stardust red. I was closer to Bowie than ever…and you *made* me do it!

As Quentin memorably quips in *The Naked Civil Servant*,

Exhibitionism is a drug. You get hooked.

While I was unable to dress myself in any outfit other than school uniform, and I was closely monitored to ensure that there would be no repeat of my grand entrance into a house of worship, I had made my stand.

Even though my face remained unpainted for a little while longer, the memory for all that had witnessed my little parade would last longer than the finest waterproof mascara.

No-one ever hit me after that.

Come out, come out, whatever you are...

No member of the LGBT community will ever forget the moment that they came out. We remember the place, the time, and the person who was the first one on earth to hear us say that simple sentence that had taken all those years to pluck up the courage to say...

I'm gay.

After the most dismal set of O-level results – a testament to the fact that I had spent most of the previous three years concentrating on staying alive rather than studying – I chose an escape route in the shape of History of Art as one of my A-level options, which meant a thrice weekly visit to the nearby Cheltenham Ladies College.

Whilst just as strait-jacketed with the same pointless rules and regulations, the Ladies College was a considerably friend-lier environment than its male counterpart. I was called by my first name in class for the first time since the age of seven, and it was an amusing change to walk along the corridors of the school to a chorus of girlish giggles rather than snarls of male aggression.

In the land of famine, a crumb is a feast.

Not only did I enjoy the subject, but I also relished the few hours of escape from the abuse, which had now shifted from physical to verbal. I was now too big and senior to hit, but I was still an easy target for those dunderheads who get a thrill out of telling someone what they already know they are.

Inevitably, my visits to this new sanctuary led to fraternising in between the lessons, which in turn led to weekend meetings in the town, and gradually to some good, albeit wholly platonic, friendships.

And then, there was Vanessa, who was, without a doubt, the most glamorous girl in the Ladies College. Blonde, blue-eyed and beautiful, with an equally attractive younger sister and a father who was very big in poultry.

We had met while doing a school play and got on ridiculously well. At the risk of sounding vain, I was getting more than my fair share of unrequited attention from a lot of the young ladies, and maybe she felt the need to confirm her superiority as the hottest catch in College by linking arms with the subject of so many wasted daydreams.

We would meet up in and around the College, and on Saturday afternoons in the town, we giggled up and down the Promenade, amusing ourselves at the mystified reaction that we were eliciting from passing College boys, who could not understand why this angel in *Gucci* was hanging around with the school poof.

Why were we so close? Quite simple. We got on. We enjoyed each other's company, we made each other laugh and, as vacuous as it may sound now – but oh so important to a teenager – we looked good together.

Of course, there was the as yet undiscussed and undisclosed matter of my sexuality. Vanessa, like every one else at the Ladies College, the Boys College and possibly the whole of Cheltenham town had heard the rumours. But being friends with someone who was a tad unusual, an oddity, even a rebel, is all very attractive when you live in a world where everyone looks the same, talks the same, walks the same and thinks the same.

One Sunday autumn afternoon, I walked the leaf-strewn lanes to St Margaret's house to see Vanessa before returning to the dark confines of College. Life was as good as it could be under the circumstances. I was studying subjects I enjoyed and had a small but sympathetic group of people I could almost call friends.

As the sky outside darkened, Vanessa and I snuggled down on a set of floor cushions and started our traditional round of gossip and giggles. She lay facing me, her cowl-necked blue mohair jumper framing her face, the heady smell of her trademark *Opium* scenting the air.

She started quizzing me about what was being said about me, and asked me if was there any truth in it.

I hesitated. I had never lied to Vanessa. I liked her too much to lie and I trusted her. My guts started to churn, my heart began to beat a little faster, my throat tightened. I couldn't look at her.

She moved in for the kill... *You are, aren't you?*

And this is the moment that, if you've never had to do it, you will never know how it feels, but I'll try...

The words rise up from the very centre of your being.
You cannot stop it.

Everything from your past, every name that you were ever called, every self-protective lie you ever told, every blow and kick you ever took, every unspoken love you ever had, every doubt and fear, everything that forced you to lock down your heart and padlock your mouth, all of it is broken open and freed by those frightening, fabulous words...

Yes. I'm gay.

I had just come out.

Vanessa squealed, grabbed my arm, and started to interrogate me.

When did I know?
Probably forever.
What had I done?
Nothing.
How did I know if I hadn't done anything?
Because…you just do.

The questions kept on coming. Her excitement meant she barely noticed her shell-shocked and newly confirmed gay best friend shaking slightly with the enormity of what had just happened. It's all very well coming out, but this was one little genie who was never going to get stuffed back into the bottle.

As we said goodbye, she gave me a big hug. I had, of course, made a heartfelt request for her to keep our conversation secret, and she had sworn to do so. But as I walked home, shivering in the evening air as the night closed in, I knew that it was only a matter of time before this private admission became common knowledge. It would come as no great surprise to anyone, but it was a confirmation of their suspicion and then the law would be taken into their own hands.

It took a few weeks.

Vanessa told her best friend, who told *her* best friend, who happened to mention it to someone who had a boyfriend at College.

The deed was done.
The rope was cut.
The dogs were unleashed.

I was alerted to the oncoming storm in a note from a girl friend, begging me to meet her at the gates at the end of the final lesson of the day.

She told me that the news was out and everybody knew. I walked into the evening meal that night, and yes…everybody knew.

Eyes glared at me. I heard the comments I was used to, but they were now said with a knowing authority and added menace. I walked with my tray of food towards my traditional table. Those whom I could call my friends were already seated, not meeting my eye and looking clearly uncomfortable. I knew that if I joined them they would be cast as gay by association as my *bum chums*. I took their cue, and found myself a place, alone and away from everyone, eating my meal with as much measured dignity as I could muster. When I could take and eat no more, I stood up, walked towards the doors, deposited my tray, and fell out into the darkness.

How was I going to survive the rest of my time here?

I survived by keeping my head turned, but not and never down. I walked the routes to and from school that no-one else took, so that I would not have to be stared at and passed by in silence. I spent as much time as I possibly could in the safety of the town and in my favourite cafes. I had a total of five people that I could still call friends, who stood by me.

But I was eighteen, I was out and I was proud, and it was the most wonderful feeling.

I had to come out many times after that. Each change of school, each new set of friends, each job…it never ends.

But, once you're out…you're never in again.

The Quentin Crisp of Sidcup

I remember seeing an interview with Boy George at the height of his fame in the early Eighties. Ever the media darling, he was having a fine old time of it, trying to educate some cheesecloth-shirted presenter that dressing-up was all a part of our history and heritage.

Look at our nation! he exclaimed. *All those powdered wigs and all that make-up, we were all drag queens!* Once television was around for a few more decades, people wouldn't be so shocked by the sight of a man in make-up.

There had always been freaks, we just couldn't see them. When we did, there would be a nationwide rising of the great exhibitionists, and someone would stand up and say, *I'm the Quentin Crisp of Birmingham* or *I'm the Quentin Crisp of Leeds*, and it would be a cult.

I was the Quentin Crisp of Sidcup.

Being away from home and a drama student gave me a complete licence to be whoever I wanted to be.

The now permanent mask of make-up was teamed with crimped and coloured hair, a collection of diaphanous scarves and whatever clothes I could lay my hands on that I was certain most other men would never dare to wear. It was fun riding the bus to college with the secondary school kids, all open-mouthed at this human rainbow that was travelling with them.

I may have got stared and shouted at, but just as in the aftermath of my grand entrance into the Cheltenham College Chapel, I knew why and I didn't give a damn.

Occasionally, I would get a lovely and ticklish reaction my appearance. Riding on a boat up to Hampton Court, wearing a jacket weighed down with safety pins, chains, badges and medals, some giddy old girls took a great interest in my outfit. Marvelling how long it had taken me to construct, one of them fingered the collar lined with hundreds of tiny safety pins and said to me, conspiratorially, *Well, I know where to come if me knicker elastic goes!* before collapsing into gusset-busting giggles with her equally helpless companions.

I loved her.

In the summer of 1987, there was an announcement in the paper. Quentin Crisp would be presenting his one-man show at the Donmar Warehouse in Covent Garden.

This was an evening not to be missed.

This was my opportunity to pay homage to the man who had opened up the make-up box, unlocked the wardrobe door, released the latent wit within my soul, and who had provided me with the armour I needed to charge into battle with my oppressors…in other words, come out of the damn closet!

My guru was coming to town.

I bought my ticket, sat in the front row of the balcony, primped and painted, dressed in my student-chic satin and tat, and awaited his arrival.

The music of a string quartet faded and onto the stage walked this small, slight man wearing a pastel-green suit, a cravat, and a fedora tipped gently to one side. His face was powder-white, with rouge on his cheeks, mascara on his eyes and lipstick in his mouth. He carried a cane, which he placed by a hat stand, and then turned to face his audience…

It was an audience with history.
My history.

He delivered his show with measured aplomb. It was clearly rehearsed down to the last word and gesture, but then as he had previously stated in an interview *You say what you have come to say.* Nothing was left to chance.

All the famous anecdotes were there. *Never ever try to keep up with the Joneses. Drag them down to your level. It's cheaper.* And my personal favourite and daily mantra *Other people are a mistake.* He told tales of Eva Peron, and Joan Crawford, stories of the stars of the silent screen and the downtrodden tramps of London. He presented his guide to life, the *modus operandi* that he had created and used to get from one place to the other as safely as possible, never looking at or speaking to anyone unless they demand that he did so.

As the interval approached, he announced *They will be bringing out a selection of my books, which they will encourage you to buy, and which it would be my pleasure to sign.*

Being both a poor student and an ardent groupie, I had come prepared with a copy of his latest book, *Manners from Heaven*, already tucked in my pocket, with the logic of *first in the queue, longer to talk.*

As the other members of the audience perused the book shelves, I approached the desk where he sat alone. He looked me in the eye and smiled. A gentle, slightly world-weary smile, and said *Hello.*

I presented my book to him, admitting that I had brought along a previously purchased copy. As he signed it, he said

Very sensible, I would have done exactly the same.

And that was it.

I was aware that there was already someone behind me, clutching her book and eager for a brief exchange with the author and I duly thanked him, said goodbye and made way for the next person.

I stood to one side, at a distance, watching as the queue formed, as books were signed and the adoring crowds returned to their seats, clasping their autographed treasure.

What do I wish I had said?

Thank you?

Maybe *Mr Crisp, you changed my life… well, not changed but influenced… affected… informed… no, changed…*

Or how about *You gave me the courage to explore, to discover, and to stand up and declare who I was, at the most testing time in the most horrific place.*

Even *You're my hero, and everything I would like to be.*

But I didn't tell him. The moment was gone and would never happen again. Ah well…

After the interval, during a section when he answered invited questions from the audience, he was asked who he feels now that so many people want to meet him, after so many years living on the outside of society, and he responded with a tried and tested pearl of wisdom

Never try to join society. Stay exactly where you are, and let society form itself around you.

Then he told a particular story about an encounter with someone who, just like me, wanted to meet him.

Having moved to Manhattan, Quentin Crisp offered an open-door policy to his life. All were welcome to call and visit him in his increasingly filthy flat, which he never cleaned, claiming that *After the first four years, the dust doesn't get any worse* and that his ambition was *to meet everyone in the world…and I'm not doing too badly.*

He then told us of a young girl who visited him, a girl still living at her family home, who was exhausted from being on the receiving end of pointed barbs from her parents.

She, like me, had been to see and meet Mr Crisp, with a book to be signed.

Having acquired the autograph, she looked at it and said *I'm not quite sure whether to show this to my mother or not.*

She was, he declared, *going to save it for her darkest hour. When her mother says 'You dress yourself like a harlot, you do nothing that your father wishes, you use this house like a hotel', the girl is going to say 'Mother, you don't know the half of it. I've met Quentin Crisp'."*

And so have I.

Pass it on, boys, pass it on...

If someone had told me that twenty years after leaving the classroom as a student I would be returning as a teacher, I would have laughed in their face.

I never trained nor qualified as a teacher, but – courtesy of a degree in Theatre Arts – I found myself employed as a permanent supply member of the drama department in a rough, tough secondary school in Bexley

As I sat in the car park on my first day, a good hour before the school even opened, I said a prayer to whatever entity might be listening...*Please let me me be a good teacher. And help me make sure that no-one has to go through what I did.*

It took all of five minutes to realise that I wasn't in Kansas anymore.

On the hour, every hour, thirty children would come into my classroom, check out the new teacher, and work out ways that they were going to break me down.

By the final period of the day, when it had gone round most of the school that there was a new drama teacher, male, who probably worshipped at the same church as Dale Winton, I was wise to the game and ready to roll.

In they came. There was an atmosphere I can only liken to that scene in *Oliver*, when the orphans have drawn a straw and someone is going to ask for *more*.

As I concluded taking a register, a hand shot up, and this perfectly cylindrical boy with the devil in his eye, said *Sir, I know I'm going to get in trouble for this, but...are you queer, Sir?*

I looked out at the room.
Thirty pairs of eyes looked back.
And I thought…what would Quentin do?

What did he say? *Never admit or deny.*

So, I looked the young man in the eye, smiled, and said
Why? Are you interested?

Half the room gasped.
Half the room laughed.
Well, I thought, *if I have a reaction, I must have their attention.
So, shall we get on with the lesson?*

It worked. Not always, but usually.

I learned how to deftly remove *he* from any discussions about my personal relationships, and made the decision to keep my private life private. I wasn't back in the closet, but just wearing a scarf of safety.

But, as we know, honesty is always the best policy…

I was out on the town with a particularly lovely group of Sixth Formers, enjoying a day out at the Globe and an evening at the National Theatre. We were all sat by the side of the Thames, talking about everything and nothing in particular, when the subject of my apparent popularity as a teacher came into the conversation.

I parried away the compliment.
I don't know about that. I think most people think I'm a big poof.
One of the students asked, simply and directly
Sir, are you gay?

And, just like before, the only answer to rise up was the truth. *Yes, I am.*

They were, predictably, all totally lovely on hearing a confirmation of what they already knew.

As I reflect on a fifteen-year career in the classroom, I am proud of many things.

I am proud of working alongside children who found my classroom a place of absolute safety, where they could explore their imaginations and unleash their creativity.

I am proud of directing an edited production of *Bent*, and presenting it to an audience who would never have seen the like before in their lives. As a dear friend who saw the perform-ance remarked *I cannot believe I have just seen a production of 'Bent', in Welling, with most of the audience in tears.*

I am proud of writing and and hosting an annual celebra-tion of diversity to the entire school, in which I reminded them of how dull the world would be if we were all the same, of how the ignorant use of inappropriate language is not only hurtful but damaging, and that we must never forget or ignore the contribution of gay men and lesbians to the world.

But, more than all of this, I am proud of all the young men and women who plucked up that particular courage to come in my room for *a chat.*

As I watched and listened to these young men and women creeping out of the shadows and into the light, vomiting out those life-changing words, I felt a sense of purpose that far outweighed any round of applause on a stage, or any other accolade or award.

On my last day as a teacher, as I sat in my garden with a dear friend, halfway through the third bottle of champagne, I remarked that I had made it through the day without shedding a single tear, which is most unusual for me!

As if on cue, I received a Facebook message from an ex-student. He told me how he had heard my assembly at school, and knew that he was not alone. How he had seen me walking round the school, watching how other people reacted and related to me in such a positive manner, and realised that being gay would not lead to being a social outcast. How he had told his family about who and what he was, and how wonderfully supportive they had been. How, on his first Pride march that year, he had followed the theme of that year's festival and nominated me as his hero.

And then I cried.
No, I didn't cry. I sobbed. Great big Disney tears.

I was now officially one of the stately homos of England.

Just like Quentin Crisp.

Sign here, please!

Brief encounters
with Broadway Babies

Confessions of a stage-door stalker

I have done my fair share of star-stalking in my time.

In those distant days before the mobile phone camera in your pocket, if you wanted to prove to your friends and even to yourself that you had met somebody famous, the only goal in town was to get their autograph.

Signed photographs – either genuine or the handiwork of a fan-club secretary – were regular competition prizes and a much-sought holy relic for the crazed teenybopper.

It brought you just a little bit closer to your idol, because you were holding something that they had actually touched and, if you imagined hard enough, you could *feel* them on the paper.

But waiting outside a stage door can be an embarrassing experience. The derisory looks of passers-by, their smirking faces a palette of mockery and pity, and the greatest insult: when your patience goes unrewarded.

I remember standing behind the Dominion Theatre after a musical called *Time*, starring former teen idol, David Cassidy. As a fifteen-minute wait became thirty, which in turn became forty-five, the crowd steadily diminished to the hardy faithful few, shivering but still clutching their programmes as tightly as their dreams of seeing David.

And the bastard sneaked out the front.

Adding an autograph to a photograph, a programme or record sleeve can be financially very rewarding.

Squiggles from all four Beatles could set you back £12,500, while Billie Holiday or both Carpenters are a steal at £1,750. A Presley autograph will cost you around £3,000, Sinatra clocks in at £1,500 while a scrawl from Streisand is a mere £300, a fact that will put that famous nose totally out of joint.

Showbusiness is big business, but for the devoted fan, money is no object, and I am sure there is a *Phantom* fanatic somewhere who would empty their piggy bank for the libretto signed by both Michael Crawford and Sarah Brightman and collected by yours truly on the night the record hit the racks.

Maybe fewer would be interested in my precious copies of albums by David Sylvian, Prefab Sprout, Elton John, Rufus Wainwright and Everything But The Girl, all autographed and acquired at *HMV* or *Virgin* in-store signings in those halcyon days when London still had record shops.

There are certain signatures that I will never part with, and each of these treasured scrawls is accompanied by a story.

Four Broadway legends coming up!

Antici...pation!
The day I met Tim Curry

How do you do
I see you've met my faithful handyman

I was a *Rocky Horror Picture Show* addict from my moment I saw Tim Curry on screen, stomping his silver-glittered heel as that sweet Transylvanian transvestite, and made regular weekend pilgrimages to the late night picture show in a flea-pit of a cinema in New Jersey, joyfully shouting at the screen, squirting my water pistol and time warping with the rest of the unconventional conventionalists. I once attended a showing at the High Temple of *Rocky* worship at the 8th Street Playhouse in New York, but I didn't dare breathe amongst that audience of resident professionals, where to get a word wrong would be akin to farting in church.

The film is a wonderfully kitsch tribute to the science-fiction and horror B-movies of the mid-Twentieth century, and is as good an excuse as any to slap on some face paint, strap on some stockings and hurl toast, confetti, abuse and whatever else comes to hand or mind at the screen.

Frank N Furter is played to the delicious hilt by Mr Curry and sets the film alive. I loved every raise of the eyebrow, every flick of the hip, and every line delivered, to quote the great man himself, *with my usual 300 pounds of condemned ham.*

Unsurprisingly, considering that there is some ambi-sexual bed-hopping, a leading man in suspenders and more than a little naked flesh on display, the film has a *huge* gay following.

It's camp, loud, funny, fantastical, and carries a message I adopted as a farewell motto of encouragement to write upon my departing students' shirts on their last day in Year 11, that tear-filled day when all is forgiven and it's all about the love love love.

Don't dream it. Be it.

Even as we age, and that pelvic thrust becomes a tad arthritic, when we forget some if not all of those classic audience-led lines, we are more Doctor Scott than Riff Raff, and we're not sure we could stay awake for a late-night picture show, this is all we need to remember…

Don't dream it. Be it.

I won't, and I will.

I was lucky enough to see Tim Curry playing Mozart in *Amadeus* on Broadway in 1981, and the following year I saw him in *The Pirates of Penzance* at Drury Lane, giving a performance almost as outrageous as his Frank N Furter, bouncing off strategically placed springboards and prowling the stage like a panther on heat.

Clad in britches so tight that you could see every sinew, whipping his rapier out at any given moment, he was sex on legs, still in magnificent voice, with that rich chesty baritone filling the theatre, wringing every drop of humour he could out of every word in every line.

I had to meet him.

I took my place amongst the crowd outside the stage door, ready for the main man. Out he came…and he was so small! Lovely, and more than willing to sign my programme, but… small!

Now I understand those heels.

Mama dearest
The day I met Liza Minelli

We gay boys do adore our divas, and no-one is more adored than Judy Garland. So, come on, you Friends of Dorothy, let's take a ride along the rainbow.

Judy was the daughter of a gay man, and possibly the wife of one as well. She enjoyed the company of homosexuals, much to the chagrin of her handlers, and her latter-day concerts became an often ecstatic bonding between artist and her male-dominated audience. The love and devotion for this incredible woman erupted into anger on the day of her funeral on June 28 1969, when the customers of the openly gay Stonewall Inn, situated right in the heart of Christopher Street in New York City, decided that enough was absolutely more than enough, and responded to yet another police raid with a riot that trumpeted the beginning of the battle for gay rights.

But what is it about Judy Garland that makes her such an icon to so many gay men?

Some will say it is all down to Dorothy, and those ruby slippers that led us down a road of dreams to a place where we could be free. Others would put it down to her many rises and falls from grace, how she would soar like a sequinned phoenix from the ashes of her own self-destruction, and triumph over adversity. Maybe it was all down to the fact that she sure knew how to belt out a good tune.

I think it is because she sang love songs to and about men. When you fall in love, or are thrown out of love, when you are either too elated or too upset to articulate the feelings in your heart, you need a song that expresses how you feel. When you can't give someone anything but love, or you wish that you were alone together and that the one you adore would just do it again... you let Judy be the messenger.

At drama school in the Eighties, living away from home and at last at liberty to discover the bright lights of the West End of London, I would often head into town on an early evening train. Dolled up to the nines and armed with my faithful *Walkman*, I would listen to a homemade cassette of the classic 1961 Garland concert at Carnegie Hall, often described as *the greatest night in showbiz history*. As the train pulled into Charing Cross station, I would look across the river and see the twinkling lights reflected on the Thames, dreaming my dreams about meeting a man on the Trolley, who would make the strings of my heart go *Zing!* and who eventually, inevitably, would be yet another man that got away.

I never saw Garland in concert, but I have seen enough footage to be able to imagine what it would have been like to breathe the same air as that tiny woman with a voice that shared the very stirrings of her soul, and who ran the entire gamut of emotions within each and every line that poured out of her.

I would have loved to have met her.

I have met her daughter, the deeply damaged – but remarkably still living – legend, Liza Minnelli.

I was a guest at the annual *Ivor Novello* awards, always deliciously star-studded and swanky affairs, attended by all the very top names in the music business, which allow a wonderful opportunity to schmooze and stalk the ever-so-slightly off-duty celebrity, and offer a fascinating insight into the intrusion and the occasional sheer bloody rudeness that these singers of songs have to tolerate.

One year, an announcement asking the crowd of cameramen surrounding one table to leave Elton John alone so that he could eat his lunch in peace.

Another year, a thundercloud of rage crossing the face of Ray Davies, lead singer and songwriting genius of The Kinks, as he was barged out of the way by hordes of photographers, clambering over everyone to get a snap of Bros, who were slap bang in the middle of their fifteen minutes of fame.

On this occasion, having done her duty and presented an award with her usual gush of showbiz hoopla, Liza Minnelli was standing amongst a crowd of cameramen, clinging for dear life – and good photo opportunity – onto the arm of Paul McCartney.

As they faced a barrage of exploding flashbulbs, I wandered over and waited patiently for the assault to stop before moving in to get a quick squiggle as a souvenir.

I mean, come on, McCartney and Minnelli? How often does that happen?

Paul was all thumbs aloft, *wa-hay* and *love love love* for everyone. The occasional lead singer and co-songwriter of the most successful group that there will ever be in the history of pop music, with a bank balance that made all the other personal fortunes in the room look like pocket money, was disarmingly relaxed with all the attention and pleasantly polite to all.

And, so…Liza.

As she signed *Love, Liza* with an elaborate flourish, I thanked her for the joy that her music had brought to my life. I wasn't lying. Just as her mother had given me a musical shoulder to lean on, so Liza had blessed me with *Maybe This Time*, that hymn to eternal optimism, and hell, if it all went wrong again, what is life, but a cabaret, old chum.

As I rounded off my little gasp of gratitude, she raised her head and looked at me with eyes the size of *Wagon Wheels*, seized my arm and schaid, most schinsherely, *Thank you, scho much*, as if I had just volunteered to give her my kidney.

Bless her. She just *needs* to be loved and she learned that from her Mama. And who better to supply that love than an audience full of gay men?

Liza is a big belting, shoe-stomping, work-up-a-sweat showgirl from the old schoolhouse of stars, and her shows – just like Garland's – with all that showbiz pizzaz, are not a million Prozacs away from group therapy.

I saw her show at the London Coliseum in 2008, when she was in great shape, in great voice and in between marriages, or as she put it *44 pounds and one husband lighter*.

The fagerati were out in force, and tumbleweed was blowing through a deserted Soho, where some poor drag queen was belting out *I'm one of the girls who's one of the boys* to two bored members of staff and a confused couple on a city break.

I have never seen a performer who quite so adamantly demands that her audience not only love her, but must unite as one to help her get through the show. No matter how many times she gushed how terrific *we* were, it was our job to return that feeling with interest at the end of every song in the form of her all-healing drug of rapturous applause.

At times, it was like watching a Garland tribute act. She has acquired and adapted all those trademark nervous tics, the laughter-choked stories, the *schincherity* of every darn moment, and it would be easy to lay the bulk of her fame at her Hollywood lineage. But when she pulls up a chair, and the spotlight hits her, those eyes look to the gods and she purrs out

Maybe this time, I'll be lucky, maybe this time he'll stay

it's worth the entrance fee for that moment alone. Just like Elaine singing *Memory* or Barbra singing *The Way We Were* it's a song that belongs to just one woman.

After a wall-tumbling version of *New York, New York*, belted out to the balcony and complete with three thrilling key changes, she slumped on her barstool, a shimmering mess of sweat and sequins, and gasped out to us that she would *remember this night forever*. I doubt if she could remember her way backstage by this point, but that made no never mind. The bears in the front row had tears running through their beards, and we all stood and cheered as she drank in the love that she craves with every fibre of her being.

Diva.

The faggots' favourite
The day I met Barbara Cook

Just as you can tell someone's age by their *Blue Peter* presenter or their *Doctor Who*, you can tell a gay man by their diva.

There are the grey-haired survivors who prop up the bar of *City of Quebec*, still devoted to Dorothy Squires and Shirley Bassey, the bathhouse babes who worship at the temple of Bette and Barbra, the soul queens who adore Diana and Whitney, and the muscle-Marys getting down with Madonna and Mariah.

All tough and talented women who have taken an industry located right at the epicentre of a man's world, and who have harnessed the power and enduring adoration of the men who like men to make them not only equal, but queens of all they survey.

In the latter years of the Eighties, I was introduced to the work of the godlike Stephen Sondheim when I was shown a documentary about a gala recording of his musical *Follies*. Among a stellar collection of Broadway legends, was a woman by the name of Barbara Cook.

Not only had I never heard of Ms Cook, but I had also never heard the song *Losing My Mind*.

A relative newcomer to heartbreak, with only one of note under my belt, I felt my soul explode as I watched and listened to this woman, dressed in a sequinned lilac gown, with a spot-lit halo of blonde hair, caressing notes of almost unbearable beauty out of her body. With apparent ease, but surgical detail, she sang of the all-consuming insanity of grief that follows the end of a relationship. It underlined the lesson I was learning by the minute, that when love goes wrong, every waking moment is governed by thoughts of the one who has just left your entire world in disarray.

By the end of the documentary, I had fallen in love with the composer, the show, the song and the singer.

By beautiful coincidence, she was just about to play some concerts at the Donmar Warehouse, and I was lucky enough to attend.

I had never heard a voice like it. I had never heard anyone interpret lyrics the way she did, with absolute commitment, truth and understanding, singing songs that I had heard many times before, but making them seem new, fresh, alive and relevant.

When she announced a six-week run at the Albery Theatre the following year, I took full advantage of the student-standby ticket policy and went every week, repeatedly finding myself seated in the front row, much to my delight and her mystified surprise, as she looked down at this young man on yet another return visit.

Reading the programme, I noted that her final Broadway appearance had been in a barely-known musical entitled *The Grass Harp*, based on a novel written by Truman Capote with music by Claibe Richardson and book and lyrics written by one Kenward Elmslie, an American relation and a renowned poet and performer.

I had an opportunity to meet Kenward, and I will always regret not accepting his invitation to join him at a club in Greenwich Village for what he described as *raffish entertainment*. I was barely 18 years old at the time, had only been in the States for a fortnight at the beginning of a year in a New Jersey

High School, and was still finding my feet. Such a shame, as I think we would have got along well, both being pink sheep of the family.

Armed with as good an opener for conversation as anyone, I went along to meet Ms Cook at a signing at *Tower Records*, a multi-floored palace of music that looked down over the madness of Piccadilly Circus.

I stood in line with all the theatre queens, all chattering about what they had seen, what they were about to see and what they would emigrate to avoid, and waited my turn to meet this Broadway legend and my latest love.

As she signed my poster and record, I informed her of my family tie. She looked up, her cherubic face full of joy, and said *Oh, Kenward, he's a DEAR man. Aren't you lucky to have him as a cousin? And isn't he lucky too! You're a dandy fella!*

She was so lovely.

A few years later, I went on my now annual pilgrimage to see Ms Cook in concert in the wood-panelled walls of the Barbican, arriving at the venue with a good hour to spare, and aimlessly wandering the carpeted labyrinth, burning up the minutes until showtime.

Lady Luck led me downstairs to the bowels of the building, and I heard a piano tinkling through the closed door of a rehearsal room. A voice joined in, a voice I knew so well. Barbara Cook was warming up her pipes.

With no-one around to stop me, I sat by the door and listened intently as she ran through some of the numbers to be featured in the evening's programme. As I heard her voice caress the beautiful Bernstein melody of *One Hand One Heart*,

I was reminded me of a quote from the maestro himself regarding songs and singers, that I had read on the sleeve of her album *It's Better with a Band.*

> *What is a singer? Someone who has the talent, the voice, the intelligence and the technical dexterity to convey all of the above to the mind and heart of the listener. Who is a singer? Barbara Cook, that's who.*

He knows, you know.

Two hours later, I snuggled into my seat, feeling terribly smug that I had got a few more minutes of music for my money.

She was flawless, as always. All my favourite numbers were there, sitting pretty alongside numbers that I had heard others sing, but never really appreciated until Ms Cook took every line, every note, and every moment in-between and held you in her majestic hand.

And then, a delightful surprise.

I'd now like to sing you some songs from 'The Grass Harp', written by Claibe Richardson and Kenward Elmslie.

As I sat in the audience and heard her sing *Chain Of Love*, I felt an overwhelming sense of familial pride.

> *If love is a chain of love,*
> *as nature is a chain of life*
> *With link after link after link*
> *Then I'll always be in love, I think.*
> *No youth ever stole my heart*
> *No suitor ever sought my hand*
> *I've nothing at all to confess*
> *Yet, I've always been in love, I guess.*

The song finished and the audience burst into applause, and I hoped that the cousin that I never met, that *dear man* still living in the heart of Greenwich Village, still writing and reciting his poetry, could somehow hear it, and know that this English Elmslie and fellow pink sheep had just found another hero.

I sang a duet with Barbara Cook at the Haymarket Theatre.

That's a lie. I shouted at her. But she asked for it!

Late September 2004 at the aforementioned venue, we're about five songs into the programme and everything is going swimmingly, with our heroine in fine voice, interspersing each number with warm and witty repartee.

The next musical cab off the rank is *I'm In Love With A Wonderful Guy* from *South Pacific*, a regular childhood listen which had become an adult favourite and – on that enchanted evening – an actual reality as a wonderful guy from San Francisco sat holding my hand in the stalls.

The Hammerstein lyric is an exuberant expression of the elation of love, and the words tumble over each other as the character finds unashamed joy in being *as corny as Kansas in August, high as a flag on the Fourth of July.*

Unfortunately, on this particular occasion, it's not so much as case of tumbling as stumbling. She hits the opening line of the rarely sung second verse and her mind goes blank.

I've been known to da da da da…

The words have gone.

She turns to Wally, her longstanding accompanist, who is helplessly vamping away at the piano. He doesn't know either.

Let's have another go.

I've been known to…da da da da…

It's not working.
She turns hopefully to the audience.

Anybody know? she pleads.

Now, I can't bring myself to shout out *Behind you!* at a pantomime, but this was too magical a moment to miss. From my seat in the stalls I shout out *share your satirical attitude.*
Without dropping a beat, she picks up the cue, sings the line, adds a perfectly syncopated *Thank you!* and finishes the song, giggling with relief and to tumultuous applause.

As we clap our congratulations, an elderly lady in the neighbouring seat turns to me and smilingly says *You're too young to know that song,* and tempted though I was to treat the house to my shower-time serenade of *I'm Gonna Wash That Man Right Out Of My Hair,* I content myself in the tiny knowledge that I can now happily lie to myself and say that I sung a duet with Barbara Cook.
And for that, ma'am, and for soundtracking thirty years of my life with your beautiful work…thank *you.*

There was another Broadway legend who sang one of cousin Kenward's songs, appropriately titled *I Trust The Wrong People.*

What was her name again? Oh yes…

Elaine Stritch.

Broadway Broad
The day I met Elaine Stritch

*Good times and bum times, I've seen them all
and, my dear, I'm still here.*

So sang the legendary Elaine Stritch, standing on the spot-lit stage of the Shaw Theatre in the autumn of 2008. She was in her early eighties, but still wearing her favoured stage outfit of a simple white shirt and black tights, with her immaculately coiffed blonde hair framing her face, every line a testament to a life not so well, but mostly truly and absolutely lived.

She looked as good and sounded as great as she had ever done, a showgirl and a star, right to the end.

As she reeled off Sondheim's witty list of trials and tribulations both suffered and survived, I wondered if she was ever tempted to include some of her own chapters from the diary of her life. Like working with Ethel Merman and Noel Coward, going on a date with Marlon Brando, dumping her longtime lover for no-hope homo, Rock Hudson, or knocking back a drink or twenty with Judy Garland at a post-show party.

Or working all the hours God sent to claw her way to stardom and then, without warning, finding herself sitting and waiting for the phone to ring, or defeating alcoholism and promptly developing diabetes.

Good times and bum times? She'd seen them all, and she was still here.

When she introduced the song, she noted – with her distinctive rasp adding a slice to every word – that she had heard women in their sixties sing *I'm still here*; on several occasions, women in their fifties sing *I'm still here*; a few times, even women in their forties sing *I'm still here*; before drily asking *Where have they been?*

Until you have lived, loved, lost, struggled, succeeded, sunk but somehow survived, you haven't earned the right to sing that song. A bit like writing your autobiography before you hit twenty-five, a current fad about which I'm sure Ms Stritch would have had something to say.

She had something to say about everything.

One of my pet peeves, and a crime for which I believe there is no adequate punishment, is talking in the theatre. If I have paid for a ticket to see a show, I want the experience to be absolute and undisturbed, and not to have my evening ruined by a running commentary from the person sitting behind, in front or anywhere near me.

If this occurs, the offender is usually given three warnings. Starting with a straightening of the back, then a sharp look over the shoulders, and finally a full turn round and a wide-eyed stare of warning. Only if all this fails do I actually say something.

Stritch is onstage and somewhere someone is talking, but when I turn around I cannot see where the constant chatter is coming from. I'm not the only one looking for the source of the disturbance, as the whole row have their heads on revolve. Who the hell is responsible for this constant and deeply irritating interruption to the evening?

Only towards the end of the show do we discover that the guilty party is two lads in the lighting booth, perched above the stalls, who have no idea that their conversation is bleeding out and down onto the audience.

This innocent error, however, does not stop me from heading hot-heeled over to the house manager at the end of the show, dramatically declaring that our evening has been totally ruined. He is most apologetic, and offers us a free drink at the bar as a peace offering.

As we are standing in the foyer, knocking back the complimentary Merlot, he walks over to me and asks if I and the other members of my party would like to join a *meet and greet session* onstage with the Broadway Baby herself. It would have been churlish to turn it down, so we return to the now empty auditorium, thrilled at the prospect of meeting a true star of the Great White Way.

Standing on the stage, with three other small pockets of people – who have no doubt paid a mint on top of their tickets for this privilege – we are informed by an assistant that Ms Stritch is just having her insulin shot and then she will be with us.

Five minutes later, the side curtain is pulled aside and out walks this little old lady.

Where is the upright, spotlight-loving, all-singing, all-dancing teller of caustic and witty tales?

Where is the star that has kept us all enraptured and hysterical for the best part of two hours?

Who is this frail woman, wearing a large and shapeless peaked cap, with tinted glasses the size of soup bowls, thin as a rake and creaking across the space that she has owned so magnificently for the past two hours?

It is Elaine Stritch.
Tired, grumpy, grouchy, gravel-voiced Elaine Stritch.

And she is not happy.

Although the bulk of the audience have gone home, she still has to put up with these damn people who have too much money in their bank accounts and nothing better to do than try to get a little bit more of her.

So, let's make it brief.

She comes up to us, holds out her hand, and firmly shakes each of ours in turn, while barking out, in that unmistakable rasp, *Do I know you?*

And she didn't.
Of course she didn't.
How could any of us know Elaine Stritch?

We were just a small group of hangers-on, getting a little more than our money's worth, and all she wanted to do was go home.

What Lily did

The day I met
Paul O'Grady

There was a boy, there was a girl

In September 1984, on my first day at the Rose Bruford College of Speech and Drama, located in an old country house in Sidcup and hidden away in the leafy enclosure of Lamorbey Park, I wandered down the driveway, as lost as a puppy. As I rounded a corner, I saw a young woman, walking assuredly across the campus, sporting a bright purple beehive. A kindred spirit, I thought. I plucked up the courage to ask her the location of wherever it was I was supposed to be. I was duly informed and, after that briefest of conversations, we went our separate ways.

That was the day I met Katrina.

We were in different years, and on different courses, but in a college the size of RBC it was inevitable that our paths would cross again. Katrina was one quarter of an all-woman singing group called *The Hot Doris Band*, the stars of any college cabaret, but having heard me playing the piano in a portakabin, she suggested a collaboration.

The first number we ever performed together was *I Say A Little Prayer*, and I remember sitting behind the piano, listening as she belted out that Bacharach and David classic, thinking...*this woman can sing!*

After three years of College, I was fortunate enough to land my first job – and the hallowed Equity card – with Proteus, a community theatre company in Basingstoke, and enjoyed a succession of varied roles, starring as a faithful dog, a tortured writer, a teen idol, and in a final burst of glory, a pantomime dame.

I look a bugger in a dress, but I'll do anything for money.

When I heard that I was to play the dame, I instantly thought of Christopher Biggins, an actor born to play the part of the traditional big-bosomed and bonneted widow, all wrapped up in layers of fabric, flounce and fun, who provides the lynchpin between the action onstage and the audience.

The director had a surprise for me up his sleeve.

No, dear, I don't want you to be a dame. I want you to be a drag queen.

Up to this moment, the only men I had seen making a living out of dressing up as a woman were Danny La Rue, Hinge and Brackett and Dame Edna Everage, all of whom would baulk at being labelled drag queens, probably preferring the term *'female impersonator'* or *'gender illusionist'*.

The nearest I had ever got to seeing a bona fide drag queen was at Pride 85, when I stood with the crowds on the South Bank and watched Divine, bumping her hips and shaking her blue-sequinned belly, while singing *Shoot Your Shoot* on the deck of a tugboat and sending a tidal wave down the Thames.

Once again, the director threw all my preconceptions out of the window.

I don't want you to be grotesque, darling, I want you to be glamorous. I want you to be Grace Kelly. He promptly produced the costume design, a 1950s swing dress in Pepsodent pink satin, a big flower on the breast, blue tights, three-inch heeled white stilettos, a feather boa, with the whole confection crowned by a blonde bob wig.

Learning how to walk in heels took three days, but by the end of the nine-week run, I was jiving away without a care in the world. I also learned that being a man in a dress is an incredibly empowering experience. While no stranger to make-up, which was now as routine as a roll around the pits with a deodorant, I have never been remotely tempted to look like a woman.

A man onstage in a dress who is very clearly a man can get away with almost anything. The children laugh, the women empathise, and the men willingly surrender to being the object of a one-sided desire, safely protected by the footlights. Pantomime is playtime, and anything goes.

Between acting jobs, I made ends meet by playing the piano in restaurants and hotels, accompanying the chatter and clattering cutlery with a selection of easy-listening standards and showtunes. Occasionally I would slip in jazz-infused versions of *Keep The Red Flag Flying* and *Sing If You're Glad To Be Gay*, to check if anyone was listening as they chomped down their chicken, but my musical humour always went ignored and unappreciated.

Indeed, the only time I was ever acknowledged was when a drunk punter, invariably male, usually dressed in a brown leather blouson jacket and beige slacks, would stagger up to the piano in a haze of Remy Martin, lean in and slur the desperately unoriginal and incorrect quote from *Casablanca*.

Play it again, Sam.

Much as I wanted to say the line was *You played it for her, you can play it for me…play it*, I just smiled as if he was the first to ever whip that quip out of the witty bag, played the damn song, and nodded beguilingly at the brandy glass on the top the piano, stuffed with two five-pound notes. I played it for you… now pay for it!

Just as I was deliberating whether to head to the Edinburgh Festival and play the lead in the jazz musical *Downtown Uproar,* a role which could prove to be either a big break or a career killer, I got a call from Katrina.

We had stayed in touch after leaving the cotton-wool comfort of RBC, and met up for the occasional night of drinking and dancing at *Heaven* and the Albany Empire in Deptford. We had been invited to perform a thirty-minute set of songs from the Great American Songbook at the annual Summer Ball of the gay night *Outdance*, which proved to be enough fun for both us and the audience to prompt a return visit the following year for a Seventies-themed Summertime Special.

It was fun, but when it was done it was done.

Katrina was a damsel in distress. She was in a show, someone had dropped out, it was a month away from opening night, and the director was desperate to find a replacement. *Come on, darling*, she said. *It's one song, two performances, it'll be fun.*

The show was *Wednesday Matinee*, a musical written by Eric Presland, and David Harrod. The piece was set in a run-down cinema on a rainy afternoon in the early Sixties, and featured a motley crew of locals, gathered together to escape from the rain and, in some instances, from the drudgery of their life.

The cast was an assemblage of Presland's pals from the gay scene and cabaret circuit, all individual performers in their own right, including Katrina, on an extended sabbatical from *The Hot Doris Band*, and a character called Lily Savage, the creation of one Paul O'Grady.

I was to play the part of a teddy boy, which was convenient, as I still had my quiff from my recent role as a teen idol and a pair of bright blue suede brothel creepers, which I had worn in the show and – conveniently – forgot to return on the last night.

117

My song was a mercifully short mid-tempo rock'n'roll ditty, with the rather uninspired chorus of *I'm a greaser, I'm a greaser, I'm a greaser*, meaning that I had to take care not to sound as if I was singing a love song to that cow of the concentration camps, Irma Grese. Diction, dear, diction.

The object of my character's attention was Dolores, the terminally bored usherette, played by Lily – or Paul – and I think we were included to provide some heterosexual counterpoint to the rather disturbing back row fumblings going on between the school boy and the dirty old man.

I was introduced to Paul, and we set about trying to make something out of this number.

I had never heard of and certainly never seen Lily Savage, and it was hard to imagine this skinny, sandy-haired scouser, wearing a nondescript jumper, blue jeans and always sucking on an ciggie, done up to the nines in full drag. Paul was quiet, a little withdrawn, even slightly ill at ease, and rehearsals were quick to the point of perfunctory. It was a case of learn the words, sing this line to the audience, sing that line to Dolores, bump and grind a bit, and there you go. As I gyrated around the stage, giving it my best Shakin' Stevens, Paul shuffled from foot to foot, chewing gum in time to the music. A few rehearsals and we're done.

The show was booked to play one night at the now defunct Diorama in NW1, and one the following week at the Albany. It was decided that, as the musical barely lasted an hour, the opening half of the evening would be 'party pieces' performed by the company and it was revelation for me to see work that had been doing the rounds in a world that I never knew existed.

It made sense for Katrina and I to do something together, and we locked heads and humours to come up with something suitably silly.

I'm not sure how many packets of biscuits we consumed before we struck on the idea of Julie Andrews having a crack at *Time Is On My Side* including a little snippet of *Poppins* for added nonsense. Blame it on the Bourbons. Our musical madness gave Katrina the chance to be a little Mary and for me to release my inner Dick. For our second number, we chose to reprise our successful finale at the Albany and close our ten minutes on the stage with our ticklish take on *Puppy Love*.

The opening night at the Diorama was the first night that I met Lily Savage.

As we returned to the communal dressing room, with the positive reception to our party piece echoing behind us, there she was...

Flames of blue-and-white eyeshadow licked around eyes framed by lid-breaking lashes and high-arched brows. The mouth was lined and lipsticked. The heeled shoes and the mountainous blonde wig, with a front crest of dark roots, added height and power. The slim frame, now enhanced with padding to create bust and ass, was wrapped in a fitted pink usherette's uniform, with a small hat nestled amongst the curls. She looked regally imperious and deliciously common.

Savage looked at us through a haze of *Lambert & Butler*, and said

You should do that on the circuit. They'd love it, honest to God.
(Erm...what is this circuit everyone keeps talking about?)
Tell you what. You get yourselves a keyboard and I'll get you some gigs.

Katrina, anxious to move on from *The Hot Doris Band* and find a new musical partnership, was all for it, while I was excited by the prospect of working someone I already admired as a performer and adored as a friend.

I was also more than a little terrified. I was unaware of – and thus very unsure about – this circuit and scared of taking a leap into the absolute unknown, especially as I was accustomed to the comfort of a contract, dates in the diary, regular pay, and was forging a decent career as an actor.

A decision was taken, a phone call to a disappointed director was made, and we took our first steps on the journey into the twilight world of gay cabaret.

I bought a Yamaha keyboard with a decent piano sound and enough drum beats to keep me happy and we set to work searching for songs that we could mould into a show. We found common ground with the female icons of the Sixties, Disney, corny country and western, witty show tunes and the classic songs of the Seventies that soundtracked our formative years, with the modus operandi of *If it makes us laugh, chances are they will laugh with us.*

The name of the act can be credited to Katrina's mum, the lovely Valerie. She was fully acquainted with her daughter's band of merry men, and would always enquire after our general health with the question *How are your boys?* And there you have it. *Katrina and the Boy*, with not a *Wave* in sight.

On September 2 1990, we made our debut at the Comedy Cafe, a cosy little venue tucked away on Rivington Street in East London. The room was full of long wooden tables and benches, with a menu packed with bean sprouts, lentils and chickpeas, aimed fairly and squarely at the *knit your own yoghurt* brigade. The stage was small but serviceable, as was the sound system, but it was a safe place to cut our cabaret teeth. We filled the room with friends, who laughed in all the right places and joined in with any audience participation that we foisted upon them.

At the time, there was a plethora of free gay papers to be found in the pubs and clubs. *Capital Gay* was the big read in London, the *Pink Paper* was a nationwide publication and *Gay Times* was still available, despite the concerted efforts of that witch, Mary Whitehouse. *Boyz* had just made its debut, and there was the occasionally glossy like the short-lived *Vada*, which blessed us with a very kind review from our Comedy Cafe show, praising the *indomitable Katrina and her ever-faithful and subservient Boy*, and saying that we were *not only nice to listen to, but nice to look at... a refreshing change to the usual acts.*

After a few more shows at the Cafe, Katrina called Savage, telling him that we were good to go.

The call was returned by his partner, Brendan Murphy, with a booking for Saturday night, or rather Sunday morning.

1am at the Royal Vauxhall Tavern.

There is a tavern in the town

A little history lesson for the uninitiated.

The Vauxhall Tavern was built in 1863 at Spring Garden, Kennington Lane, on land which was part of the Vauxhall Pleasure Gardens. Originally a music hall, the tavern became a favourite haunt of returning servicemen and local gay men, who were drawn to the entertainment provided by the small-but-perfectly-dressed troupe of female impersonators, and it remains London's oldest surviving gay venue.

The good, the great, the bad and the lost have all passed through the doors of this historic hall – including a man-dragged Princess Diana smuggled in one night by Freddie Mercury and Kenny Everett – and there can be few fledgling drag acts who did not dream of one day holding court on the stage of the RVT, praying to survive the experience and live to fight another night.

In a city of constant change, with a skyline scarred with cranes, The Tavern stands defiant, like the House of Clennam in *Little Dorrit*, with no buildings either side to support it, and you can almost see the walls bending in the wind, trembling with the vibration of the passing traffic. The windowless exterior, splattered with posters, looking not dissimilar to the *Camberwick Green* musical box, only adds to the intrigue and secret mystery of what lies within.

The blood burgundy paintwork and the huge mirrors create the eerie atmosphere of a Victorian house of horror. The bar extends the entire length of the right side of the bar, facing out onto the floor, which is peppered by columns, hopefully holding up the nicotine-stained ceiling. To your left is a raised level with a wooden balustrade, lovingly nicknamed *The Muppet*

Gallery. A DJ booth is tucked in the corner, next to the steps leading to the dressing room, and on the rear wall, flanked by two boards announcing the entertainment for the week, is the stage, hidden behind bright red curtains.

You have arrived at the Palladium of drag.

The two hymn boards bore names of the Vauxhall legends who held residence, including the holy trinity of the top drag queens in town.

> *Monday:* Her Imperial Highness and Empress of all Russia, Regina Fong.
> *Thursday*: 'Stars of the Future', hosted by Our Lady of Vauxhall, Lillian Maeve Veronica Savage.
> *Sunday:* the Super Destroyer Adrella, the firm but funny headmistress of 'Sunday School'.
> *Saturday:* the early show starred the much-beloved stalwarts Lee Paris and Jimmy Trollette, and for the late show, a new name on the board...

Katrina and the Boy.

We arrived at the Tavern just as Lee and Jimmy were in the final furlong of their act. I stood by the side entrance, my keyboard wrapped in a bin liner and tucked under my arm, watching as two men in their mid-fifties, shimmering away in sequinned tops and satin skirts, with painted faces and hairspray-encusted wigs, led the beer-fuelled crowd in rabble-rousing choruses of *Sweet Caroline* and *Delilah* and thought that this must be what a rugby club looks like after a home win. As the two sweat-drenched drag queens launched into their final number, my heart started to thump in time to the beat of their discoed-up version of *No Regrets*, and with my stomach on final rinse and spin, the clock ticked inexorably towards the hour of judgement.

There was little enough space in the dressing room for two people, let alone four, so we waited until Lee and Jimmy had come down the stairs to be surrounded, hugged and loved by a crowd of admirers. Once behind the door, we looked at each other, silently acknowledging that we were both scared to death. I went onto the stage, now shielded by a curtain, and set up the keyboard, while Katrina got herself pressed, dressed and ready for battle.

John Charles, the resident DJ, whose sallow complexion and sunken eyes made him look like a Dickensian undertaker, came in with the microphones and asked if we had any special sound requests. We decided that loud was the best option. Hopefully we could beat the audience into submission with the sheer power of volume.

The minutes ticked away. No going back now.

1am.

OK, ladies and gentlemen, welcome back to cabaret at the Vauxhall Tavern and tonight we have a brand new act, making their debut, so please put your hands together and welcome... Katrina and the Boy.

The curtains opened to scattered applause and a pub-load of people looking at us. I hit a descending semi-tone chord riff, now forever associated with *The Phantom of the Opera* and we launched into our opening number, a swinging version of *Cruella de Ville*.

As chorus followed verse, you could see the confusion rolling round the room...

That's a real woman. Yes.
Is he going to take his clothes off? No.
WHAT IS THIS?

This, my darlinks, is cabaret!

One number down and Katrina started on her mission of making best friends with everyone in the room. We led them out of the middle of nowhere with a little Dusty, walked them after midnight with some Patsy Cline, and got some singing along with *What's New Pussycat*, with the applause and laughter growing louder and longer as the set rolled along. The more dextrous drinkers even joined in with a silly little hand-jive that we had created to accompany the chorus of Helen Shapiro's snappy little take on Neil Sedaka's *Little Devil*.

We hit the final note, I bounced up to the front of the stage to join Katrina for a bow, and looked out a collective of smiley happy people.

Somehow, we'd got away with it.

Encouraged by the response and calls from the DJ, we return to the stage for an encore. As I play a gentle underscore, Katrina invites the audience to assume the role of a sad, lonely, spotty and socially inept teenager, locked away in a sock-scented bedroom, with only their own body odour and a crusty old record player for company, their poor excuse of an existence only given meaning by the fact they worship *her!* With this image and this emotion in mind, she then encourages the assembled mass to *respond to this song as you see fit....*

And they called it...puppy love.

It starts with a little squeal, somewhere out in the darkness.

Someone, somewhere, gets what we want and joins in with the spirit of the song. Gradually, more people start to emulate that teenage hysteria we've all seen but thought that only young girls were allowed to express. But, we're in the Vauxhall Tavern now. Fuck it!

> *Someone help me, help me,*
> *help me please.*

Now, it's getting fantastically ridiculous. Big, burly, check-shirted men, clutching a beer in one hand and stretching the other towards the stage, are gleefully screeching away, singing along with this cheesy old classic, and loving every minute. We end the number, join hands, bow, and head back to the dressing room, look at each other and burst out giggling.

That was fun!

There's a knock on the door. It's Savage. Unbeknownst to us, he's been watching the whole shebang from his personal pew in a darkened corner of the Muppet Gallery.

Ay, what did I tell you? They loved it. Fucking loved it. Honestly, that was great, just fab. Good on ya both. And I tell you what, if you can work in front of this fucking shower, you can work anywhere.

Well, we'll see about that.

We started hanging out together, with Savage, in his role as the roaming hostess, blowing the clarion call and introducing us to the dives, divas and doyennes of the twilight world of the homosexual.

One evening, we were all snuggled a red velvet banquette in *Madam Jo Jo's*, the infamous Raymond Revue bar in the heart of Soho, being plied with drinks by the beautiful

Barbettes, the stunning transvestite waitresses who worked the floor under the watchful gaze of Jo Jo herself.

Ruby Venezuela, the resident drag queen was onstage, in all her glamorous and grotesque glory, getting to grips, in no uncertain terms, with a gondola's pole. For a little lad from Surrey, who had never set foot in a burlesque bar, it was all one hell of an eye-opener.

In walked Jeremy Joseph, now one of the most powerful club promoters in the West End and owner of the *G.A.Y.* brand, but at the time a DJ at the Royal Oak in Hammersmith. Savage called him over.

Jeremy, this is Katrina and the Boy. You need to give them a booking.

Jeremy looked at us for what we were, an unknown entity, and dared to hesitate...

Don't fuck around, Jeremy, give them a fucking booking, And none of that midweek graveyard shite either. Saturday night or nothing.

We got the booking. You didn't mess with Savage.

Within a few weeks of our debut, we were invited back to join our new friend and mentor at the RVT for the launch of a new Thursday night show, and for what was to prove to be an unforgettable evening.

Thursday night at the Tavern was traditionally billed as *Stars of the Future*, featuring a drag-bag of hopeful and occasionally hopeless amateur acts, all desperate for a little bit of attention and applause. After years of hosting this weekly assault on the senses, Savage was ready for something new. He christened the night *Workers' Playtime* and asked us to join forces with the very glamorous and deliciously Jewish Dave Lynn to launch the new evening.

We arrived at 10pm, in good time for the 11.00pm kick off. The place was already packed, with a heady buzz of anticipation in the air. Savage and Dave were in the wardrobe that masqueraded as a dressing room, play-fighting for space in front of the mirror as they applied the warpaint, sharing stories of recent experiences in venues they both knew, and engaging in some light-hearted bitchy banter.

Suddenly, without warning, the lights went out, and the pub was plunged into silent darkness.

A phone call to the LEB brought the news that there had been had been an electrical fault at a local building site, and that, hopefully, the power would be returned in fifteen minutes. Fifteen minutes became half an hour. Meanwhile, the confused and bemused punters stood in the slowly fading glow of the emergency generator lights. A box of candles was found and distributed around the bar, adding to the monasterial atmosphere, while two drag queens and a double-act sat in a pitch-black dressing room, wondering if the show really must or even could go on.

A voice shouted out from behind the bar...

The tills are down, but if you've got the right money or you don't mind not getting any change, you can get a drink.

The punters seemed content with that, and weren't inclined to leave and head home. They'd come out for a show, and a show is what they wanted. Backstage, Savage went into full Gracie Fields mode and rallied the troops. The DJ was dispatched to a local garage to pick up enough batteries to power up the keyboard while Murphy rooted out the megaphone used on the annual Sports Day, and found a torch with enough oomph to light up enough of the stage.

The four of us circled up and thought of songs we all knew that we could pull off without any rehearsal. The trivial matter of no light and no sound was not going to stop us. We were all experienced performers. As Gracie would say

Hee hee, come on, lad and lassies, the factory's open again!

Big Ben chimed out midnight, the curtains opened and four shadowy figures walked out onto the stage to a roar of appreciation from the assembled throng. We heaved ourselves up to the very lip of the stage and, after a welcoming rant against the LEB from Savage that could probably be heard in the Outer Hebrides, we launched into our opening number, *Da Doo Ron Ron*. The crowd sang along with gusto, drowning us out completely, but that was the point. If we were going to make this work, we would make it work together.

Katrina had a big voice which could hit the back wall without the aid of a microphone, and gay men do love a belter. Dave was an established and favourite performer on the scene, and led the community singing an ear-busting *Hava Nagila*.

But, even with all this extraordinary business going on, I will always remember this night as the first time I saw Lily Savage on stage. This was *his* pub and these were *his* people, and the adoration that the crowd felt for him/her was overwhelming.

I sat behind my keyboard in absolute awe, rocking with laughter, watching this vision in leopard print mini-skirt and white thigh boots regaling the audience with her surreal tales of shoplifting and soliciting, her incontinent sister Vera, her children Bunty and Jason, and the trials and tribulations of Queenie, her pet whippet. It was a seamless stream of cider-fuelled consciousness, delivered in a *Woodbine*-rough Liverpudlian accent, that left you both breathless and begging for more.

An hour later, four slightly huskier-voiced performers bowed to the overwhelming cheers from the crowd, and retreated to the haven of the dressing room, promising to return in a fortnight, only this time with power.

The bizarre events of the night made the gay papers, with praise for the *troupers* and likening the night to a good example of gritty Brits and *the spirit of the Blitz*.

There was a Blitz going on. The community was at war with an invisible and life-threatening enemy.

I had seen the advert, and listened as the voice of John Hurt grimly intoned about *a deadly disease that affects us all and there is no known cure*, watching as a chisel carved *Don't die of ignorance* into a headstone. I had also seen Larry Kramer's brilliant play *The Normal Heart* at the Albery Theatre, and heard the woman sitting behind me pass comment on the collage of headlines about HIV/AIDS which covered the set, with a toffee-toned sigh of *Oh, that's terribly oppressive*. I'd heard of empty seats at the Palladium production *La Cage aux Folles*, with the production struggling to stay afloat in the light of this new wave of fear and homophobia.

But I had never met someone living with the disease.

I was, to all intents and purposes, a gay nun, having only ever slept with one man, with the world of pubs, clubs, cottages, saunas and cruising areas all uncharted islands.

I knew nothing, but all that was to change.

The more shows we did, the more people we met, the more I realised that this disease was running rampant through the community, laying waste to a whole generation. I became too used to meeting men, from their twenties to their fifties, all of whom defiantly announced that they were living with this disease, not dying from it. They spoke honestly and candidly about their status, as if talking about it was a personal therapy, a means of removing both the stigma and the fear. Talking about it, and sometimes laughing about it, which we know can be a darn good medicine.

In these times of trouble, the cabaret acts became the tonic for the troops. We realised that it was part of our job to raise morale, to spread a little happiness and create a breathing space where we could all just let go and forget, even if only for an hour or two.

In the fallout from the charity-drives of the Eighties, we were painfully aware that if you wait for financial support from governments, chances are you will just keep waiting. We had to look after our own. The diary began to include regular benefit evenings and fund raisers, and we were more than willing to join the front line at shows organised for the Terence Higgins Trust, the London Lighthouse and Body Positive.

One such evening took place at the Players Theatre, a quaint venue in Villiers Street, that still played host to the *Late Joys*, a celebration of the golden age of music hall. As the West End audiences were heading home, and the hard-core clubbers were staking their claim in the queue outside *Heaven*, those in the know swept through the doors of the Players and settled down for an evening of truly old-fashioned entertainment, led by a master of ceremonies, with a cavalcade of performers and some good old-fashioned sing-a-longs, including *Oh, the fairies, OH, the fairies!* which was sung lustily by certain members of the very mixed audience.

The show was titled *Not a Command Performance*, and was to play for one night only.

The evening was compered by the leading light of the cabaret circuit, Ms Lily Savage, revisiting her dark roots as hostess of *Stars of the Future* as she presided over a hysterical on-stage episode of *Stars in their Eyes*. The contestants included Millie Mopp, a gloriously kitsch cartoon gutter-mouth, screeching her way through *Wuthering Heights*, Adrella performing his legendary Liza Minnelli impersonation to *Losing My Mind* – barely visible behind clouds of some very suspect white powder – and the disarmingly handsome Paul Adams sweetly duetting with '*the skinny bitch*' Tzarday on Jason and Kylie's *Especially for You*.

What I remember most from that night is the backstage camaraderie, the genuine affection between the acts, the sound of laughter, and the humbling knowledge that we were doing something, no matter how small or how silly, to ease the suffering of people who just got unlucky. Illness, disease and death do not discriminate, but somehow the human race tends to take up the cudgel of fear and ignorance to persecute, bully and belittle those who are fighting for their lives. This time, we were fighting back.

We were a family.

As well as furiously trying to keep our respective shows fresh, Savage and Katrina and the Boy still found time to combine forces and work on material to tickle our audiences at *Workers' Playtime*. A plot was hatched to rehearse and present *You're Just In Love* from *Call me Madam*, a duet culminating in a complicated vocal counterpoint. My snug little maisonette in Lee was elected as the rehearsal space, and I hope the neighbours were entertained by the laughter, swearing and occasional singing bleeding through the walls as we battled to make the number work.

At the time I had an inexplicable crush on a certain Geordie footballer who had wept into his England shirt and won the hearts of a nation gripped in the patriotic fever of the 1990 World Cup. While loathe to plaster my tiny but tastefully decorated home with pictures of my latest crush, I *had* sneaked a few pictures of the man onto my bathroom wall, prompting a tea-relieving Savage to scream *Argh Ian. Why the fuck have you got Gazza on the wall? Christ alive!*

Don't hate me. I just can't resist a man who cries.

We only did the number once, but it was a hoot. I think even the irascible Ms Merman would have approved.

On our increasingly rare nights off, we would try to catch each other's shows, which usually concluded with a lengthy lock-in after hours. One very late evening at *Recession*, a short-lived club in Russell Square, one of the chosen few who had gathered for a nightcap let slip that he had never seen *The Sound of Music*. And so we did it for him.

The sight and sound of Savage giving his finest Mother Superior, with a bar-towel wrapped around his head and crooning out a nicotine-laced *Climb Every Mountain* would probably have encouraged the most fervent nun to quit the convent and go find herself a nice Captain. It was all such fabulous fun.

That New Year's Eve, Savage invited us to join him at the Tavern, warning that the evening was always *a wild one*. That turned out to be the understatement of the season.

By 10pm, the bar was already rammed with happily refreshed revellers, though how anyone managed to get to the bar and buy a drink was a minor miracle. We battled our way through the crowd and fell into the relative space of the dressing room.

Savage was halfway through his preparations, mock-moaning about the night ahead, before introducing us to the other *cab of the rank*, as he used to call the acts. Tillie was another daughter of Liverpool, with a mischievous pixie face and a wicked sense of humour. He had been a regular at *Stars of the Future*, delighting the audience with his superb staging of *The Lonely Goatherd*, skipping over the stage and almost knocking himself out with two enormous blonde plaits in the process, while making a mockery out of the fact that his legs were both bound in callipers.

At 11pm, the curtains opened. The crowd roared like they'd seen a winning goal at Wembley as they welcomed *our Lil* onto the stage. Savage launched into his opening number, a lacer-ating rewrite of Peggy Lee's *I'm A Woman*, before unleashing his brilliant comic brain and delivering line after line of wicked wit and belly-laugh gags.

Tillie put his number one crop to comic use and mimed to Sinead O'Connor's *Three Babies*, wrapped in a white sheet and clutching two hairless baby dolls, while we pulled the big guns out of our sing-along songbook, and were rewarded with the best male voice choir in town, singing and swaying away to *It's Getting Better* and *Georgy Girl*.

It is always a joy to join forces on stage, and Savage decided that we should be Tillie's backing group on his breakneck version of the country-and-western classic *Rocky Top*. Katrina grabbed a spare wig, I contented myself with a tambourine, and Savage set up shop behind my keyboard, pursing his lips and reeling round on the piano stool, arms flailing like Bobby Crush, not touching a note, but giving it his all, as the crowd pogoed up and down like Laura Ingles on acid.

There was not a spare square inch of floor to spare, and those lucky enough to get a drink placed their glasses on the lip of the stage, where they were knocked over by the heaving crowd, sending pints of beer flooding over the stage. Murphy demanded a mop from behind the bar, and made regular attempts to keep the spillage away from the leads and pedals, but to no real effect.

As the bells welcomed in 1991 and we all joined an onstage conga, we must have looked like four Gene Kellys, splashing around in puddles of *Carlsberg*. I looked out at the mayhem below me, holding tight to Savage's waist as we danced our way into the New Year, and allowed myself a moment of reflection...

It had been an eventful year, which had seen me make some decisions, take some chances, and trust my instincts.

From pantomime dame to lounge pianist, from phone calls saying *Yes* to phone calls saying *No*, from a terrifying debut to a delightful success in the end of year Reader's Poll in *Pink Paper*, which awarded us with *Best Cabaret Act*, it had been an incredible ride.

I gave thanks to whatever strange forces and twists of fate had brought me here.

And I also thought...*If my mother could see me now!*

Out, about, and on the road

One stupidly early morning in March, Katrina and I boarded a coach bound for the Library Theatre in Manchester to take part in a Stonewall fundraiser: *Thespian Tendencies*. Our fellow passengers included Sir Ian McKellen and Michael Cashman, who had co-ordinated the event.

The evening, which also starred the regal Pam St Clements, the joyfully jolly Sue Johnston and some very noisy Brooksiders, was a great success and, after the quickest of backstage parties, we all settled back onto the coach to wend our way back to London.

One of the lesser-known members of the company was a little too keen to keep the applause for his performance warm on the way home, parading the aisle of the coach, fishing for compliments. McKellen, who had heard the laughter coming from the naughty boys and girls on the back seat, came down to join the party and, watching this display, leaned in and mischievously whispered in my ear, *Twinkle Twinkle...LITTLE star.*

That's the way to do it.

Buoyed by the success of the *Command* performance, the producers decided to gather the gang together for another fundraiser – unimaginatively titled *Not Another Command Performance* – to be staged on Easter Sunday at the Playhouse Theatre, which at 1,200 seats would be the biggest live audience that most of us would have ever seen.

As we all gathered on the stage for a day of rehearsal, there were many very wide and terrified eyes looking out and up at the rows of plush red seats, which climbed from the stalls to heights of the upper circle.

It was a far cry from Black Cap in Camden.

The show opened with Millie Mopp rising from the middle of the stage, his two-foot beehive leading the launch through clouds of dry ice, before breaking into his fabulously filthy rewrite of *Vogue* – sassily titled *Blokes* – surrounded by a bevy of barely-dressed chorus boys. You could feel the audience willing the performers on, with each act greeted and rewarded with warm applause.

Lily, Regina and Adrella ripped the place apart with a stomping version of *You Gotta Get A Gimmick* from *Chicago*, Savage revelling in each burlesque bump and demonstrating his limited but gloriously entertaining cornet skills.

Katrina and the Boy decided to acknowledge the theatrical surroundings by presenting our tribute to child stars who had their big break playing the coveted role of Annie when they were ten, and then sadly never worked again. The song was a gentle tip of the hat to *Forbidden Broadway* school of rewrite. Katrina did a sterling of job of setting up and singing this amusing tale of woe of dreams, delusion and disappointment, and our efforts drew some hearty laughs and cheers of approval at the end of the number, which was both a delight and a relief.

We were still a very new act – though enough people in the audience had seen us perform in the pubs and clubs to know the *Little Devil* dance routine – but nothing prepared me for the thrill of looking out and seeing a whole theatre flapping their hands, pointing their fingers, and making *bunny ears,* right from the front row to the back of the gods. As we came out for the final company bow, to be greeted by that lovely crescendo of clapping that we all crave, I knew that something very special was happening.

That night – along with good reviews in the gay press and our growing reputation as an act – caused the phone to ring and the diary to fill. The big four in town, the Vauxhall Tavern, the Two Brewers in Clapham, the Royal Oak in Hammersmith and the Black Cap in Camden were all now regular bookings. Manhattans in Earls Court, The White Swan in Rotherhithe, affectionately known as the *Mucky Duck*, the Greyhound in Slough, the Noah's Ark in Windsor and Regents in Islington were added to the rota. The Gloucester in Greenwich and the Greyhound in Woolwich were very welcome local gigs, allowing us the luxury of getting to bed before the dawn chorus and before long we were heading down the M25 to Brighton to play at the Beacon Royal, the Oriental and the Queens Arms, putting money in our pocket, dark circles under our eyes and many miles on the clock of the car.

But it wasn't all fun and gay games.

One evening we arrived at a venue that I have forcibly removed from my memory bank, to be greeted by a man who not only looked as though he should have been running a strip joint in Soho, but who had also made the curious decision to base his hairstyle on a bowl of Shredded Wheat. A *hair-don't*, I believe would be an apt description.

He showed us into the club, which was a symphony in chrome and sticky carpet, and listened with a face like a smacked arse while we soundchecked, before showing us into the dressing-room-come-office, which smelt of stale sausages and fresh flatulence.

Do you do any Tina Tuner?
No, sorry, we don't.
Oh. Kelly does Tina Turner. Do you do any Celine Dion?
No, sorry.
Oh. Kelly does Celine Dion. Do you do 'Gloria' by Laura Brannigan?
NO!

All together now…

I know Kelly does *Gloria!* She was singing it sixteen years ago in 1985, when I saw her do a gig at a Sunday night gay club in Chislehurst Caves, titled *C.H.U.M.* which stood for… brace yourself… *Chislehurst Homosexual Underground Movement,* a mnemonic almost as bad as *R.U.B.Y.S.* in Harlow, which stood for *Relax Unwind Be Your Self,* which none of the few punters ever really did.

Kelly had been working on the circuit for years. A spandex-clad, lace-gloved foxy rock chick with a voice that could strip the paint off the ceiling of the Sistine Chapel. She would treat even the smallest dive as if it was Wembley Stadium, giving it her all and then some. She was the absolute polar opposite of what we were all about, and obviously a big favourite with Mr Flatulence.

Tempted as we were to say *Why the fuck didn't you book Kelly then?* we bit the bullet and did the gig. We should have taken our first impression of the owner as a warning sign and done a runner. The audience were made up of a collective of disinterested twinks and drunk dykes, including one particular lager lout of a lesbian, who firmly believed that feigning masturbation in front of my straight-but-certainly-not-narrow comedy partner was somehow going to turn her head and win her heart.

As we counted the seconds until we could get off, get paid and get out, Katrina smilingly closed her introduction to the final number with a heartfelt promise that we would never ever darken their doors again.

Some you lose.

We were once, and only once, booked to play at an evening billed hopefully as *Out and Proud in Newham.* But after sneaking a peek through the curtains and spying a smattering of gloomy people nursing half a lager in a plastic cup and sitting by themselves at enormous tables, we retitled the sad and sorry event *Staying In and Not That Bothered in Newham.*

To quote Phil Starr, the much-missed queen of the one-liner, *What you must remember, dear, is that we've all left the stage to the sound of our own heels.*

Like us, all our new cabaret pals worked over the weekend, so Tuesday evening became the new Saturday night out, and we became welcome guest members at the official meetings of the *APCDQ,* aka the *Association of Plain Clothes Drag Queens.*

The venue for the gathering was usually the Star Bar in *Heaven*, a corner of that vast club where I had danced so many nights away in the mid-Eighties, while keeping an eye on the clock in order to get out of the club and catch the last train home.

The Star Bar was a much quieter part of the club and reeked a little less of spilt beer and amyl nitrate. There was a resident pianist on site, and as the hours ticked away and the alcohol started to take effect, it didn't take much persuasion to coax a number or ten out of the assembled trannies in trousers.

Some *PCDQs* wanted to keep their work persona separate and secret. On stage, Millie Mopp looked like Mari Wilson gatecrashing *The Rocky Horror Show*, while offstage John was a rough looking skinhead, all army trousers, *Dr Marten* boots and a bull-ring through his nose, and more than likely to be found cruising the dark leather-clad corridors of the London Apprentice, the Block or the Anvil. Woe betide if you called him Millie when he was out of drag. It was John. *Alright?*

Savage had no such issue. Everyone knew him, everyone called him Lily, never Paul, everyone said hello and he would always respond with a *Hiya, how are ya?* as he grabbed a drink and headed for a place to park, never standing centre stage or demanding attention.

But once he'd sunk a few pints, he needed little encouragement to get up and do a number. His favourite, and mine, was a bawdy old blues number, featured in the show *One Mo' Time*, with the superbly suggestive title of *You Got The Right Key, But The Wrong Keyhole*.

As the pianist started to roll out the slow Basin Street boogie, Savage would grab his cider, climb onto the stage, plonk himself on a chair or a block, grab the microphone and, in his best New Orleans growl and gravel, tell the tale of Liza Johnson and her thwarted lover...

> *You got the right key, but the wrong keyhole*
> *I couldn't get along with you to save my soul*
> *Last night I went down to the hardware store*
> *And got another lock for my front door*
> *I got a new man, and he's better than you*
> *He starts his loving when you get through*
> *So take my tip, honey, leave my door*
> *Because your key don't fit my lock no more*
> *I said you got the right key,*
> *but you're working on the wrong key hoooooooooole!*

On that last note, he would raise his leg and arch it over, snarling out that last note with all the guts and grime of a real red hot Mamma. It was burlesque dressed in checked shirt and jeans, but just as fabulous as if it was in fur and feathers.

I loved those evenings.

Oh, I do like to be beside the seaside

Heaven sent another lovely opportunity our way, borne on the wings of the angelic Dave Lynn.

Dave was the resident drag queen at *Heaven*, and was asked by the management to get something special together to lure the punters into the club on a Saturday evening, before the traditional witching hour of midnight.

Surprisingly enough, the winning idea was a piece of theatre. Dave called up Savage, and they hatched a plan to stage a live version of the classic 1962 film *Whatever Happened To Baby Jane*, starring those two Hollywood icons – and sworn enemies – Bette Davis and Joan Crawford.

The animosity between the two actresses was well-known, and the bad blood between them bled onto the set and into every scene, creating a fascinating piece of reality cinema. The competitive tension is omnipresent, as the two divas of the screen battle it out for centre stage. Davis goes berserk in the role of the demented former child star, tormenting her wheelchair-bound sister, played by Crawford. There are a plethora of classic lines and defining moments, often quoted and re-enacted by gay men, which would lend themselves easily to an hour-long staged interpretation, and Savage got to work, editing the script and injecting his own wicked wit.

Lily was to play the Davis role of Baby Jane Hudson, Dave was to take on Crawford's part as the sister Blanche, while Katrina would play Elvira, the faithful housemaid, and I was cast as Edwin, the pianist hired to revive Baby Jane's long dead career.

The rehearsals were an absolute riot. Savage had created a superb text which not only invited but encouraged some playful improvisation. He made no attempt whatsoever at an American accent, and hearing Davis's lines delivered in broad Birkenhead only added to the hilarity. I am not sure that we ever made it through one rehearsal without all four of us collapsing with hysterical laughter.

I had never seen the movie before working on the show, and thus had no idea of the cultural impact it had made on the gay community. The Hudson sisters were clearly great favourites for an all-male Halloween dress-up and, from curtain up, it was clear that the audience knew this film inside out and back to front.

The walls of this dark tunnel of a club, so used to being shaken by the beat of pounding dance music, reverberated to the sound of laughter.

Savage revelled in the satanic insanity of Baby Jane, while Dave was the perfect foil as the whinging Blanche, and Katrina – the solitary woman in the entire building on the mercifully extinct *men only* Saturday night – more than held her own as the long-suffering Elvira.

Playing the thankless role of Edwin did require me to accompany Savage on a delicious rewrite of Baby Jane's signature song *I've written a letter to Daddy*.

> *I've written a letter to the Social*
> *To ask them for some clothing grants*
> *I've written 'Dear Social, please send me*
> *Two brassieres, four knickers, some pants.*
> *And then there's my sister who's crippled*
> *Her beddings been eaten by bugs*
> *So Social, please send me some money*
> *And I won't spend a penny of it on drugs!'*

You try playing that with a straight face, because I sure as hell couldn't.

The response to the show was so positive that we were offered a two-night run at the Brighton Comedy Festival, to be held at the Old Ship Hotel, so off to the seaside we go.

As the *Baby Jane* show only lasted an hour, we decided to divide the evening into two halves, the first to consist of a series of solo spots and ensemble pieces, which prompted a crazy afternoon working with Dave's regular pianist, John 'Betty' Bruzon, and a drummer, resulting in an introductory medley of songs from *Cabaret*.

Savage held court for the first twenty minutes, and was on top form, delivering a masterclass in comedy, showcasing his amazing ability to swing from set patter into one-on-one chats with old friends in the audience. Katrina and I did our bit to a warm reception and Dave took to the stage, gleefully played to his home crowd, before closing his set with an announcement that he was going to be joined onstage by a special guest for a duet.

Onto the stage crept a figure, wearing a green Irish dancer's dress, white shoes and ginger wig that would have only been worn by Worzel Gummidge. It was the first time that any of us had seen Savage as anything less than a blonde bombshell, so you can imagine the reaction. Dave quickly threw on a fresh wig and top, returning to the stage to clarify the fact that they were now Elaine Paige and Barbara Dickson, and they were now going to perform that classic show tune *I Know Him So Well*.

The next ten minutes were some of the best comedy I have ever seen in my life, with Dave bravely trying to soldier on through the song, while Lily 'missed' his cues, started chatting with the front row, slyly stepped out his shoes, and sang the wrong words, even breaking into *Stormy Weather* at one point. It was hysterical.

We closed the show with a rewrite of a song that I had knocked up after an off-the-cuff comment made by Savage during a rehearsal break at *Heaven*.

One of us mentioned *La Cage aux Folles*, which prompted Savage to explode *Oh God, I hate that fucking show! Hate it! And that fucking song 'I am what I frggin' am'. Christ alive! They should be singing 'We all hate this song, cos it's so long and it's so fucking boring'."*

Now, there's an idea.

I got to work, and imagined a West End wannabe, stuck in the back row of the chorus, slogging away in a touring production of *La Cage*, done up to the nines in boas and bugle beads, tapping his toes off and singing his little heart out, and never getting noticed by anyone. There is a common misconception that show business is all glitz and glamour, but when you are easing yourself into a costume that is still damp from the night before, applying layers of make-up to skin that is sore from weeks of putting on the pancake, and all for a few moments of *en masse* clacking, you do wonder if working in the small electrical department of a well-known store isn't quite such a bad idea after all.

I played the song to the gang and they liked it enough to learn it and put it in the show. So, ladies and gentlemen, you have now arrived at *La Cage aux Folles*.

The pianist picked out those infamous pizzicato chords to herald the entrance of the *Cagelles*. With our backs to the audience, draped in whatever gladrags we could lay our hands on backstage, we shuffled in a not-quite-synchronised movement across the stage.

And then we turned to sing...

We all hate this song, cos it's so long and it's so boring
Sick of every step, three weeks in rep, ten weeks of touring
It's one show that's been done to death in ever city
One show where you guarantee your costume's pretty
Look under our glitz, stretch marks and zits
That's why we all hate this song

You could see jaws drop, hands clutching invisible pearls and hear the gasps of mock horror as this sacred cow was dragged towards its musical slaughter. All of the audience had seen the show, and a fair proportion had probably been in it at some time or other!

Each line continued to hammer home the painted nail...

I am what I am, and what I am,
and what I am is in employment
Dancing in this trash is for the cash not for enjoyment
And you think that I look as lovely as Madonna
Underneath, I'm desirable as Des O'Connor

As we raised our satin-draped arms and hit the last note, the audience clapped and screamed their approval. We were indeed what we were, and tonight we – and they – were loving every second.

The Act Two of *Baby Jane* topped the show at *Heaven* in every way. Lily and Dave were on incredible form, ad-libbing with ease, playing every moment, and working the crowd on the well-known lines, and when Savage walked up to the front of stage and said *All together, girls, one... two.. three...* prompting the entire room to shout *BUT Y'ARE, BLANCHE, Y'ARE IN THAT CHAIR*, my heart was filled with both wonder and joy that somehow... *somehow...* I was a part of this magical moment in time, and I told myself

Remember this. This will not happen again. Remember this.

High roads and low roads

There are many things that I have never done.

I have never drunk a cup of tea or coffee, I have never watched an episode of *Star Trek*, *Only Fools and Horses*, or any of the *Star Wars* films. I have never played bingo, ridden in a limousine, worn a tracksuit in the street, popped an E or had sex with a woman.

I am a great believer in doing everything once, and scold myself occasionally for not being more adventurous. I have not travelled enough, read enough, seen enough, or – possibly – experienced enough. But there are some things that I have done which I will never do again.

I will never *ever* work at the Edinburgh Festival.

As Sondheim wrote *Once, yes, once for a lark*, but once was absolutely and positively more than enough!

Not long after the success of the Brighton Festival, Savage asked us if we would like to join him as a support act during a month-long run in Edinburgh. The original plan was to take the *Baby Jane* show, but the idea was sensibly dismissed, as the appeal would have been limited and lost under the weight of such fierce competition, and it was time for Lily Savage to come out from the comparative safety of the gay-pub-and-club circuit and reach a wider audience.

Paul, Murphy, Katrina and I were to share a rented flat for the duration of the run, which was just large enough for us to find our own space. Paul and Murphy shared the master bedroom, I grabbed the one at the other end of the hall, and

Katrina was surprisingly content to set up home in what we dubbed *the nun's cell*, a windowless box next to the living room.

The communal area was rammed with the contents of a decent-sized furniture warehouse. A large sofa, two armchairs, and a dining table, more chairs, tables, sideboards, a television, and a well-worn carpet path to lead you around this antique obstacle course. The bathroom and kitchen were both walled with wood, creating an ambience somewhere between a chalet and a sauna.

Our flat was on the third floor of four, with a tiled spiral staircase providing some – only occasionally welcome – aerobic exercise. The front of the building looked out to the flats opposite and down onto the cobbled street below, while my back bedroom window allowed for something like a view out of town and towards the hills.

Braver souls than I are more than content to bunk down in one room and spend a month living inside each other's armpits. I breathed a sigh of relief at the cosy and comfortable surroundings which would be home for the month of August.

'Lily Savage with Katrina and The Boy, The Live Experience', subtitled *'A Glittering Extravaganza from The Radical Marxist Sex Kitten'* was booked to play at the very prestigious Assembly Rooms in the comparatively intimate Wildman Room, which held just an audience of around a hundred. All three of us had played to much larger audiences, but sometimes it is far more frightening to play in front of a few rather than a thousand. I had no qualms about thumping the keys and caterwauling away in front of a noisy pub of drunken punters, but the quieter the venue, the closer the focus on your flaws.

The word *intimate* was clearly not foremost in Savage's mind as he entered and surveyed the black-walled, windowless studio theatre. His unsmiling face resembled a disgruntled crow, and he snarled his displeasure at Murphy as I busied myself with setting up the keyboard.

The first person to visit us was the Health and Safety officer, who needed to check out any potential hazards, to ensure that if the audience *did* die, they would only die laughing. He checked the plugs and leads, and then turned his attention to the fire-eating section of the evening...

Savage had long practised this skill and performed it many times, always to great effect and success. It takes a lot of guts to put a flaming torch in your mouth, especially when the flame is inches away from a wig that could turn into a fireball within seconds should the two accidentally meet.

The officer inspected the props and then asked Savage to demonstrate exactly what would happen in performance. He duly lit the torches, held them at out at arm's length and said

Then I just twirl them round for a bit. That's it. A minute, tops.

Having seen this part of the show many times, I knew that a Savage minute was more like five, but the officer seemed content and the torches were extinguished. We left the studio and headed off into the town to catch a show before heading off to bed, tired, content, and ready for opening night.

The dressing room was shared by all the acts who were performing at the Assembly Rooms, but we only met the ones who were booked into the late night slot, including the guys and gals from *Stomp*, all bristly chins, unkempt hair and dungarees. The room backed onto the Ballroom, a magnificent space with raked seating and an enormous chandelier over the stage. Savage sneaked a peak through the curtains, grizzling at the beauty of this venue compared to our flea pit and – unable to stop himself – he walked out onto the empty stage, faced up to the rows of vacant seats, lifted his arms and bellowed, in his finest Mama Merman…

Here she is, boys! Here she is, world!! HERE'S ROSE!

Back in the reality of the dressing room, it was time to get ready. It was always so easy for me, pulling on my stage wear of white vest and jeans, which meant that I was ready to roll in a matter of minutes. It took Paul an hour, a pint of cider and a dozen ciggies to transform himself into Lily Savage, much to the interest of the *Stomp* crew, who were not used to seeing a drag queen prepare.

Face done, corset and costume on, boots zipped up and wig in place, Lily Savage, Katrina and the Boy walked down the steps on the Assembly Rooms like a camp *Graeae*, strutting across the foyer on the way to the Wildman room to the wide-eyed bemusement of audiences streaming into the venue to see any of the many shows on offer.

Midnight arrived. The show opened to a house that was barely half-full, with an audience mostly consisting of friends of Frank Clarke, brother of Margi, screenwriter of *Letter to Brezhnev* and fellow Liverpudlian. He had nobly decided to come along and support Savage. But even with some well-liquored laughter from Clarke and his crew, the evening was falling flat. I passed Savage as he handed the baton over to us at the halfway point of the show, and I could see in his eyes that he was not happy at all. To go from playing to adoring crowds in every bar and club in the country to three weeks of half-empty houses was not a thrilling prospect, and hell hath no fury like an unhappy drag queen.

If the audience was quiet for Savage, they were positively funereal for us. I had the easy slice of the pie, sat at my keyboard and playing a few songs, while Katrina was out front, facing a theatre of empty chairs and unresponsive faces, battling to get a laugh or any reaction at all but to no avail. I was delighted when our time was up and Savage returned to the stage, bearing his torches to present the fire-eating section of the show.

I watched from the wings as the music started and the torches were set alight, the flames lighting up the faces of the scattered members of the audience, as smoke rose and started to fill the room and the comatose audience started to stir.

Savage took this interest as a red rag to a bull and started to work the room, rolling the flames up and down his arms, whetting the appetite for the main event…

Suddenly the room was pierced by the sound of the smoke alarms. In our room, and throughout the whole venue it was a case of *Everybody out!* and we left the theatre, swept through the main doors by the rush of audiences leaving all five venues within the building.

Hundreds of people poured out onto the street, which echoed to the sound of a fire engine that had raced to the scene. As chaos reigned, I saw a leopard-skin-clad blonde being hustled into a car, and I thought to myself

Well, that will get the show in the papers.

As Joan Collins so rightly said *There is no such thing as bad publicity.* The story was all over the morning news and the 'guilty party' was the talk of the town.

All the other performers at the festival were sat at their breakfast tables, cursing themselves for not being the first to come up with the brilliant idea of burning their venue to the ground.

Fortunately, what could have been seen as a really selfish publicity stunt was acknowledged as a mercifully funny accident, and Savage worked the mass of press attention like a pro. Suddenly, every festival-goer was more than aware of this gritty Scouse scrubber, with lightning wit and a tongue like a whip, and the tickets began to fly out of the box office.

Over the next week, the crowd and the critics poured in, the latter delivering a sackful of love letters to Savage, with the occasional bit of hate-mail for Katrina and the Boy.

It's tough being a support act. You are the half-time show at a big match, the moment when everyone gets a hot dog or empties their bladder. You are not what they have come and paid to see, and some reviewers slammed us as an unwelcome interruption to the evening. One review was so unpleasant that Savage and I decided that it was best kept out of Katrina's sight, scouring every nook and cranny in and around the theatre for the offending article, and making sure that it remained hidden and unread.

Fortunately, we were blessed with a universally glowing review, praising both *the foul-mouthed observations of the shoplifting Scouse scrubber* and the *golden-voiced Katrina*, with – and I quote – *the gorgeous Ian (who also plays the keyboards)* which is a curiously unflattering summation of my abilities as a musician. But hey, I've been called worse!

Savage became the talk of the town and everyone wanted a piece of him. Invitations started to arrive to be here, be there, be everywhere, and Savage returned the favour to Frank Clarke for his first night support by agreeing to attend the premiere of his film, and we went along for the ride.

The drag was – and please excuse the pun – that everyone wanted Savage to attend these functions as Lily and in the full ensemble. This resulted in the three of us climbing into a car, with Savage dressed up to the nines, to the amusement of the local kids and the curtain-twitching horror of the lady who lived on the third floor over the street. She had twigged that her new neighbours were 'theatrical folk', but nothing had prepared her for the image of a six-foot plus blonde bomb-site wearing a black-feathered floor-length cloak, clacking down the cobbles. I don't think she moved away from behind her nets for the rest of the run.

The cinema visit was most notable for the moment when, as the lights went down, the lady sitting behind Savage tapped him on the shoulder and said, very politely, *I'm sorry, would you mind removing your wig?* Not something you hear every day.

There was quite a Pink Party going on in Edinburgh that year.

Regina Fong was also doing the season, in her one-Highness-show entitled *Last of the Romanovs*, and Julian Clary was in town, enjoying the insanity of the multitude of shows and entertainments to be found on offer and around the clock.

One afternoon, they both came over to join us for tea, creating a collection of characters that made the party in *Alice in Wonderland* look like a meeting of the *Women's Institute*. Julian was as quiet and refined as Regina was noisy and bizarre, at one point grabbing the tartan rug off the back of the sofa, wrapping it around his head, throwing open the window, and bellowing down the street in his finest Scots accent *Aggie, Aggie, come in now, hen, ya tea's ready.*

Encouraged by good reviews and incorrigible company, Savage discovered the joys of the local nightlife – and that if you really do want to wake up in a city that never sleeps, go to the Edinburgh Festival. Every bar and club seemed to have a licence that allowed them to stay open until the last punter fell out of the door, and that would usually be Savage.

Oscar Wilde once quipped *I can resist everything except temptation*, and for a good-time-gal like our Lil, temptation was on every corner.

This was how the day would roll.

Never a morning person, he would usually make an appearance at about 3pm. Dressed in a faded and threadbare blue kimono, crawling down the hallway of the flat, bouncing off the walls like a pinball before eventually finding the door of the kitchen, he would slump in a chair and light up his breakfast ciggie.

It took a brave soul to gently enquire how he was this fine morning, or afternoon...

Fucking destroyed was the usual response.

And then the promises and the resolutions would land on the table.

No more late nights, organic food, highland walks...
Yes, Savage.

He always began the evening with the best intention. As he was getting ready to hit the stage, clipping himself into a bust-enhanced corset that even he had to admit by the halfway mark of the run was 'boggin', he was adamant...

I'm not going out tonight. No way. Straight home tonight.

This resolve lasted until around ten minutes after the end of the show.

I'll just pop out for one. Just one. And that's it.

As we descended the staircase to the foyer, the scent of battle was in his nostrils.

Right, where we going?

I was usually the 'good boy' of the gang, heading home straight after the show to my virginal bed. But I do have one very hazy image of the two of us, staggering down the road at 8am, with some divine homing device guiding us into land. Just before we fell through the door of the flat, Savage decided that he was a little peckish and we lurched into the newsagent on the corner.

He may have been as drunk as a lord but he was still determined to express his appreciation to the owner of the shop.

I tell you what, love, you do the best fucking beef rolls in town. Honestly, you really do. You really really do. I told him. Didn't I? Ian, didn't I tell you? Best fucking beef rolls in the city.

And this little white-haired lady, who had been happily listening to her Andy Stewart CD, just stood there, open-eyed and slack-jawed, caught in the full blast of adoration for her beef rolls. Bless her little tartan socks.

On rare days of sanity, while Murphy and Katrina warmed the sofas in the flat, Savage and I would go shopping down Princes Street, and I would find myself dragged into a department store as he cooed over little porcelain figures of shepherd boys and frilly girls.

I was no stranger to his flat in Vauxhall, which was an Aladdin's cave of junk, junk glorious junk. But it was strange and rather sweet to watch this viper-tongued comedian, who could drink a darts player under the table, going all soppy over a blue-bonneted figurine. We would head home, sometimes grabbing a bag of oysters – or, as Savage called them, *snot in an ashtray* – with the booty from the shopping trip hidden away, in an attempt to avoid a lecture from Murphy about buying *a whole load of shite*.

One afternoon, I embraced the Birkenhead cure for grief and took to my bed.

My ex-boyfriend – who had been my first, my one and my only love for six traumatic and testing years – was getting married. It came as no real surprise. I knew that he was bi-sexual, that he wanted to get married and have children, and had been made more than aware over the course of our relationship that he would always do exactly what he wanted. I had been introduced to his fiancee and they had even invited me to the wedding. Fortunately, being in Edinburgh gave me a wonderful excuse to decline the invitation, but when the day arrived, I was not the happiest bunny in the forest.

Savage knew what was going on, and popped in to check on me, offering to exercise his skills in witchcraft to cheer me up as I sniffled into my pillow.

I tell you what, love, I'll put a hex on them. I'll curse him with a low sperm count and her with a barren womb.

I never told him that she miscarried twice.

There were many moments of pleasure among the madness. The show was nominated for a Perrier award, which I knew in my heart was all to do with Savage and nothing to do with Katrina and the Boy.

We found ourselves in august company: Frank Skinner, Jack Dee, Eddie Izzard and Avner the Eccentric. The deal with the nomination was that, as well as doing your full nightly

157

show, you also had to do a 'best bit' moment alongside all the other acts during the final week, which meant a fascinating collision in a shared dressing room.

Savage was zipping up his thigh boots as Izzard slouched in a chair, all set to go on stage in his traditional garb of jeans and a Peruvian table-cloth masquerading as a shirt. Eddie was firing off a list of questions. Where did Savage get his boots? Who made his dress? How much did that outfit cost?

As soon as Eddie left the room, Savage turned to us and said, barely under his breath...

Tranny.
No way! we retorted.
Savage repeated his opinion.
Tranny. I can spot them a mile off. Tranny, I tell ya, honest to God.

By the end of the week, Eddie Izzard had come out as a transvestite.

To this day, I wonder if our absence might have swayed the final decision away from the eventual winner, Frank Skinner. It was clear that Savage was now in 'the big league', which came as absolutely no shock or surprise. It had been fascinating to watch him grow in stature and confidence over the three weeks. He never stopped adding material to the show, spending afternoons propped up in an armchair, with a pad and pen, scribbling down new jokes and bits of banter, delivered a few hours later as if he had been doing those lines for years.

Mark Trevorrow – the Aussie comic and creator of safari-suited lounge act Bob Downe – was now a regular visitor to the flat, and an invitation for both him and Savage to take part in a charity night at the enormous Edinburgh Playhouse hatched the plan for a duet. The song chosen was *Something*

Stupid, and I was elected to be the accompanist. Sitting on the stage, looking out over the shoulders of the two bewigged figures of Savage and Downe, I could see the dimly illuminated face of my comedy partner, sitting in a stage-side box, with her nose severely out of joint.

Don't shoot me, I'm only the piano player.

On the last night, the audience was graced by the presence of my parents, who had planned a visit to Scotland to include a night seeing their youngest son at the Festival. Knowing Savage's penchant for engaging with certain members of the audience, I begged him to let them – and thus me – off the hook. He promised me faithfully he would.

Just before we come on for the final number, he starts…

OK, now, I know that Ian's Mummy and Daddy are in the audience. Where are ya?

I stood in the wings, mortified, as he quizzed my mother over where she got her cardigan, and tried to engage her in a conversation about *Coronation Street*, which she has never watched in her life, while my father sat back, smiling at this extraordinary exchange. As Katrina and I were introduced onstage, I leant into the microphone and said *Sorry, Mum.*

The closing number of the show was the only moment in the show when all three of us were together onstage, Savage out front with Katrina and I as backing vocalists, giving it our very last grind and gasp on *These Boots Are Made For Walking.* We *bop bop shoo-wah'd* away, even adding a slice of *The Girl Can't Help It*, as Lily warned the audience that *one of these days these boots will kick the shit right out of you.*

And then, after three-and-a-half weeks of battered body clocks and battered Mars bars, late nights and early mornings, laughter and tears, and a whole load of fun, it was all over…

Are you ready, boots? Start walking

Turn right, dance off, wait in the wings, check the applause, on, bow, wave, and off. Job done. Time to take down the gear, pack up and head back to old London town.

On my return home, I meet up with a friend, with the intention of sharing some stories about the experience. He takes one look at my bony frame, my sunken eyes and the aura of absolute exhaustion that dimly glowed around me and says *Go home. Eat something. And go to bed.*

Thank you, Edinburgh, it was fun.

But…never again.

We three queens

Close encounters
with queer icons

Power in the darkness:
The day I met Tom Robinson

Sometimes you have to tell someone how you feel about them. That you love and admire them, that they inspired you, empowered you, even changed your life.

Back in my schoolboy days, in the winter holiday of 1977, I wandered aimlessly down to the local village, knowing that the only shop open would be the tiny newsagents. I had no intention of buying anything, but when I entered the shop, my eye was caught by the latest edition of *Melody Maker*.

On the cover was an angry young man, his clenched fist punching the air, and a red-lettered headline: *GAY POWER!* I was curious, excited and strangely nervous, mainly about how I was going to smuggle this paper home past the all-seeing eyes of my parents. I handed over my money and walked back up the road, reading the article about this singer called Tom Robinson, who was a screaming, shouting, confrontational, angry young queer.

I read and absorbed the article, drinking in the names of organisations I had never heard of: Gay Switchboard, Rock Against Racism and The Anti-Nazi League. He looked so *normal*, and not dissimilar to the boys who were making my life a daily misery at College, all white shirt and school tie. But his uniform was decorated with a pink triangle badge, the symbol pinned on homosexuals in concentration camps, and the number 302.0 on his breast pocket, the number allocated to homosexuality under the *International Classification of Diseases.*

OK, not so normal.

His anger at injustice and inequality was palpable in the print, as was his refusal to compromise his lifestyle or his politics. I hid the paper under my jumper to get it inside the house and up to the sanctuary of my bedroom, but my heart was on fire with the promise of this brave new world that was within my grasp, if only I could find the courage.

I bought the very laddish *2-4-6-8 Motorway* single, but the one I was waiting for was the much talked about anthem *Sing If You're Glad To Be Gay*. My patience was rewarded with the release of a live EP, which included the track, and – after my initial disappointment that the song was a laid-back jazz swing affair when I really wanted a blast of rage – I took great delight in playing it loudly in my school study, with the door left wide open for all to hear.

The *Power in the Darkness* album followed, with more songs of anger and struggle, a bold clarion call to persecuted minorities to join forces and shout it loud. The album came complete with a clenched fist stencil, which soon adorned all my school books and folders, and wearing a Tom Robinson Band badge was my own personal 302.0.

Fifteen years later, in the final days of that memorable month at the Edinburgh Festival in 1991, I arrived at the Playhouse to play the keyboard for Savage and Downe. Exhausted after a long time away from home, doing weeks of midnight shows, and partying too hard, I was not overly excited about giving up an entire evening to play one song. All that changed when I arrived at the stage door, checked my name with the security guard and, as I was picking up my bag to head on in, I heard the man behind me say his name.

Tom Robinson.

I didn't even know he was on the bill!

We were shown into the communal dressing room. I picked my peg, and Tom picked the one next to mine.

Now, what do you do?

I told myself, *Look, you are here to work, he is here to work, let's be a little bit cool and collected.*
But then I thought *Sod it.*

I turned to him, opened with an apology, but then stated that I was going to have to fawn over him!
I gabbled out how important he had been to me, how he had been an inspirational and guiding light at a time of real emotional darkness, and that it was an absolute honour to meet him.

Bless his heart, he was absolutely charming and expressed his gratitude for my outpouring of appreciation.

Power in the darkness.
Frightening lies from the other side
Power in the darkness
Stand up and fight for your rights.

Boy meets boy:
The day I met Boy George

One of the wonderful things about growing older is taking the time to look back and have a good loud laugh at yourself.

I like to imagine that if all we children of the Sixties gathered together to make a collective collage of our various fashion *faux pas*, we could look at the clogs and the cheesecloth, the high-waisted trousers and the tank tops, the pleats and the padlocks, the batwing sleeves and the soul belts, enjoy a moment of blissful nostalgia, and laugh at the way we were.

It didn't matter if you got your inspiration from the pages of a magazine or the sleeve of a record, whether you chose to run with the pack or stand out from the crowd, because once you were off the leash, the only limit was how much you dared to dream.

Once you accept and enjoy yourself as a canvas for your own personal use and abuse, the possibilities become endless.

Why have brown hair when you can go burgundy?
Why stick with black mascara when you can buy blue?
Why comb when you can crimp?

Every day presents an opportunity to play, to be a different person, a new and more vibrant version of yourself, but this does takes a particular level of self-belief, confidence and courage to pull off.

In my more adventurous years, I became quite accustomed to being the object of not altogether welcome attention, when a stare would become a shout and – occasionally – a push or a punch. Elderly ladies would inform me that I was *disgusting*, my brother told me not to go to the local pub as it was *embarrassing* for him, and I was regularly stopped by the police as I traced my technicolour pathways around the leafy local villages where I lived.

One evening in early 1982, I was unceremoniously thrown out a pub that I had been frequenting for years by the new landlady, who informed me that she was *trying to run a middle class pub* and that I, quite frankly, was *not up to it*.

I never considered myself an exhibitionist and I never sought to encourage any reaction at all to my appearance, often wearing dark glasses to hide the rainbows over my eyes, not out of any sense of shame, but because I could not be bothered to deal with ignorance.

I mean…do you really want to hurt me?

I have already admitted to my absence on that seminal evening in June 1972, when a spiky-haired starman sang his rallying cry to a legion of teenagers to use it, lose it and, within the decade, boogie their own way to the top of the pop charts.

Hey that's far out, so you heard him too?
No, I didn't, dammit.

But I was certainly a witness in 1982 when the TV screen was once again filled by a face that caused jaws to drop and the front pages of the tabloids to scream *Is it a boy or is it a girl?*

Give me time to realise my crime
Let me love and steal
I have danced inside your eyes
How can I be real?

166

Anyone who was there at the time will remember the Richter-scale reverberations after the first appearance of Culture Club on *Top Of The Pops* on that Thursday evening in 1982.

As Boy George skipped across the screen, dreadlocked and dreamy, singing his gentle ode to heartbreak, you could feel the reverberations in living rooms across the country.

Boys were worried that they fancied him, girls wanted to look like him, mothers wanted to mother him, fathers wanted to bring back National Service, and only your grandmother really believed this sweet painted peacock when he said he would rather have a cup of tea than sex.

But at the heart of all this furore was an infinitely photogenic and wittily intelligent pop star, fronting a band that understood how to create great pop music, a quite unbeatable combination for a few years before the group began to beat itself up and the drugs rolled in and destroyed the dream.

The story of Boy George is a classic cautionary tale of rags to riches, of fame and failure, from a tragic downfall to a phoenix-like rise from the ashes, combining all the intoxicating ingredients of a show business legend.

In the mid-Nineties, Katrina and I joined every other queen in town at the Queen Elizabeth Hall for an evening with Magarita Pracatan, a Cuban singer of sorts who had found her fifteen minutes of fame on the *Clive James Show*. She had a voice that could curl linoleum and no musical ability whatsoever.

She would set her bargain basement keyboard to a *bossa nova* rhythm and then make a failed but funny attempt at fitting the words around the beats. No song was safe. She would take on the greats and was fearless in her demolition of their work, with Lionel Richie's *Hello* being her most infamous musical assassination.

167

As we stood in the foyer, saying hello and exchanging kisses with the assembled gaggle of gays, I noticed a man standing alone against a wall, wearing a green peaked hat and looking slightly embarrassed about being on his own.

I instantly recognised him.

I had bought all his records, seen him in concert, watched his videos, bought the T-shirts, followed his career as it flourished, and watched with sorrow as it fell apart. Of course, I recognised him. But nobody was saying hello to him. People noticed him, they even pointed him out to their party of friends, but no-one went up to him. Not anymore.

As I was standing with our group of admirers, listening as Katrina entertained the troops, I heard a voice at my shoulder.

You're Katrina and the Boy, aren't you?

I turned round, and looked into those blue eyes that had stared out the poster on my bedroom wall. Yes, it was absolutely definitely positively him. Katrina turned around, said *Oh my God!* and the three of us exchanged a few words before a very breathless man rushed over, blurted out his apology for being late, and pulled our very brief new acquaintance towards the bar.

That was the night I met Boy George.

I'm going to fast-forward over the DJ years and the fashion line, the flawed *Taboo* and the fabulous autobiographies, the great solo albums that no-one bought, the court case and subsequent prison sentence, and stop the tape on September 5th

2016 at the iconic venue, the Hammersmith Odeon, now known as the Eventim Apollo.

Boy George is back onstage with Culture Club.

Bearded, bedecked in all his fabulous finery, in husky but magnificent voice, and clearly delighted to be re-united with his band, complete with his ex-boyfriend still beating out a steady rhythm behind him on the drums.

After a warm and wonderfully nostalgic dance through those classic hits from the Eighties, interspersed with some solo tracks and new material from a still unreleased group project, it was time for the finale.

A guitarist began to strum a familiar riff to those of us in the know, and George, grinning from earring to earring, sang the opening line.

> *Didn't know what time it was,*
> *the lights were low-oh-oh*
> *I leaned back on my radio-oh-oh*
> *Some cat was laying down some rock'n'roll,*
> *lot of soul, he said...*

It was a Seventies teen queen dream come true.

How many young gay men sat in their bedrooms, poring over the lyrics of *Ziggy Stardust* and singing along with *Starman*, pulling poses in the mirror as they experimented with their mother's eyeshadow, dreaming of their escape from suburbia to the bright city lights and life of glitz and glamour?

And how many gay men end up singing that song at the very venue where Bowie assassinated Ziggy and left the aisles awash with a river of glitter-streaked tears?

169

Just George.

You see, if you work hard enough, wait long enough, and hold on tight to the rollercoaster of fame, you get to sing a song by the man who was your hero to an audience of other bedroom-bound dreamers who looked – and look – at you as *their* hero.

It's all in the width of a circle.

Love on ya, George.

G'on, wee man:
The day I met Jimmy Somerville

Another singer who sang the anthems of my brief sojourn as a gay activist was that very angry young man, Jimmy Somerviille.

I saw Bronski Beat debut their first single *Smalltown Boy* on the television show *Earsay*, and was struck to the core of my heart, not only by the brave storytelling, but also by the overtly political stance of the first pop group in my memory to open their career with a gay statement of intent.

The album *The Age Of Consent* soundtracked my first year at drama college, and while other students were popping down to the picket lines to support the miners, I was at the Piccadilly Theatre for *The Pretty Policeman's Ball*, watching Jimmy and Bronski Beat sing in aid of Gay Switchboard.

I was also at *Heaven* years later, when The Communards did their first gig, under the strict demands that the audience was 100% gay, a dictate which led to the absurd sight and sound of a very earnest young man standing by the venue doorway, armed with a clipboard, asking each passing punter *Are you gay?*

For those of us who have seen *Life of Brian*, it was one step away from *Crucifixion? Out of the door. Line on the left, one cross each* and I remain disappointed to this day that I wasn't asked to prove my credentials.

In the late Nineties, Katrina and I were honoured by an invitation to become patrons of *The Food Chain*, an amazing organisation that provides regular and nutritious meals to people living with HIV/AIDS. Led by the indomitable Liza, we were more than happy to perform at the regular Summer and Winter parties, and were even more thrilled to be asked to do some numbers with another of the patrons, who just happened to be Jimmy Sommerville.

As we were all busy working people, it was decided that we would rehearse the chosen songs of Patsy Cline's hymn to cruising, *Walking After Midnight*, and the Communards' own *Never No More* – not in a rehearsal room, but over the phone.

At the allotted time of 3.30pm, the phone in my living room rang, and a surprisingly deep voice came down the line.

Hey, it's Jimmy.

After a few minutes of giggly chatter, with all of us acknowledging that this was one *weird* way to rehearse, Katrina put the machine onto speakerphone and off we rolled.

She sang the first verse of *Midnight* and then we both looked at each other in open-mouthed awe as that distinctive falsetto seared its way down the wires and filled my living room with the voice that had sent me spinning over many a dance floor, telling me to run away, begging to be told why and feeling mighty real.

On the Saturday of the party, we drove up to the venue for the party in North London, set up, and waited for the start of the show.

Jimmy arrived on his bike, smelling sweetly of soap, all smiles and loveliness. We found a back room with a battered upright piano, and ran through our numbers, which sounded even better when we were all together and in the same room. Buoyed with excitement, I dared to venture the idea of a third song, an old Communards B-side of the Connie Francis song *When The Boy In The Heart Is The Boy In Your Arms*. Katrina didn't know it, and so it became a very gentle duet for piano and voice. We went through it once, it sounded good, and within the hour we performed it onstage.

I wish I had a recording of it, among my souvenirs.
I don't, but I have the memory.

> *So hold him tight and never let him go*
> *Day and night, let him know you love him so*
> *With the love of your life spend a lifetime of love*
> *Make him yours for ever more.*

What Lily did next

More days with
Paul O'Grady

Love and pride

Just as you never forget your first kiss, your first love and the day you came out, you will always remember your first Pride.

June 1985, I am sitting on a bench at Chislehurst station, in my tight light blue jeans and my newly acquired white vest with the *Heaven* logo emblazoned on the chest. I am nervous, excited, and a little scared.

How many people will be there?
Will there be trouble?
Am I going to get there and back in one piece?

It seems ridiculous now to believe that these were ever even remotely serious considerations, but the Eighties were not as enlightened as people choose to believe.

As it turned out, Pride 85 was about as scary as a garden fete, and not much bigger. The embankment by Jubilee Gardens was scattered with a few stalls, selling books, badges, T-shirts and various arts and crafts that might appeal to the passing poof.

A small stage was the focal point for the entertainment, with appearances by Uncle Tom Robinson and a new band called Erasure, and as I sat on the grass, watching the show, for the first time in my life I was part of the majority.

Over the years, the march got much bigger and much louder. The parade from Hyde Park became a noisy carnival of horns and whistles, cheers and chants. The good-natured and colourful celebration was only darkened by the regular shouts of *Maggie Maggie Maggie...OUT OUT OUT!* just in case we needed reminding of the enemy.

A more joyous call and response was *Give me an O...O!...give me another O...O!!...give me another O...O!!!...what does that spell... OOOOOOOH!* The sound of hundreds of men releasing their inner Liza whenever the parade passed under a bridge, by letting out a deafening high-pitched scream, always made me smile.

Katrina and I made our Pride debut in Kennington Park in 1991, appearing amongst the cream of the cabaret circuit in Lily Savage's Tea Tent. Disgusted at the disparaging blind eye turned by some overly politically-correct organisers towards the acts who had bust their bra-straps raising funds for this event, who wrongly believed that some lesbians might be offended by drag queens, Savage decided to create our little corner of the park.

Buoyed by the wildly successful *Camp Pink* gay weekender at a Butlins holiday camp in Skegness, the Pink Coats were out in force, doling out tea, biscuits and bingo cards. It was a damp day, and the soggy ground made an elegant sashay around the park in heels more akin to a hike across the Yorkshire moors, but no-one had a care in the world.

We were here, we were queer and we certainly weren't going shopping!

By 1992, the numbers of attendees had grown so great that the party moved to the beautiful Brockwell Park, a perfect location, well-served by public transport, with a natural rake sloping down towards the main stage, and more than enough space for the vast number of tents, housing everything from beat-heavy dance to heated debate.

The sun was shining, the mood was one of absolute joy and celebration, and, for the first time, I was going to Pride with a man I loved.

I had met Mike earlier that month, after a gig at the Gloucester in Greenwich, which, in itself, was unusual. I always got very shy and self-conscious after a show, often having to be dragged out of the dressing room by Katrina for some schmoozing and ego-stroking.

I had clocked him during the gig, a broad-shouldered, bespectacled man, with a very respectable short-back-and-sides haircut and the most disarming blue eyes, which kept on catching mine.

As I was loading up the car, I saw that he was standing with two friends, all looking over and clearly talking about me. I passed them on my final run into the pub, and one of the group stopped me and complimented me on the show. A brief conversation started and concluded with the handsome man with the broad shoulders and the glasses pressing a piece of paper with his phone number into my hand.

Zing zing zing went my heartstrings. From the moment I saw him, I fell.

Our first date was at a Thai restaurant in Soho, where he impressed me by ordering in perfect Thai. We spent the evening doing the 'getting to know you' dance, which was all remarkably easy, with free-flowing and interesting conversation, plenty of areas of common ground, and no embarrassing silences. I know that it is an unwritten rule that one should hold onto one's cool, and not appear too keen at such an early stage, but I am a lousy actor when it comes to hiding my feelings. I remember thinking as we said goodbye, with a gentle lip kiss in front of Charing Cross station, that I really really *really* liked him.

After a few more dates, it was time to take things to 'the next level'. He lived locally and had a car, so we decided to meet at a gig at the White Swan in Rotherhithe, and go back to his place after the show.

I am aware that in these days of *Grindr, Scruff* and all the other internet hook-up sites, this rather quaint courtship must seem and sound desperately old-fashioned. But I was – and remain – the ever-hopeful romantic, who yearns for those days when eyes meet, there's the first smile, the brave move to say hello, the first touch on the arm, the shoulder, the leg, the first kiss…the wonder of it all.

The management at the White Swan demanded that the cabaret act hit the stage at *precisely* 10.30, with a strict *30 minutes and off* order, followed by half an hour of music before it's the turn of the stripper.

It's the logic of *all the Ds*.
Drink, dance, drag, drink, dance and dick.

We had got to know a lot of the strippers who work the circuit, and charming lads they were too. Private 69, with his flat-top and camouflage trousers, Danny Boy and his dripping candle wax, and the biggest star of all, Rebel Red, with his Chippendale hair and an appendage the size of a draught excluder.

Tonight we are sharing the bill with Achilles, for whom both Katrina and I, despite having very different tastes in men, carry a mutual but well-hidden torch. He is a man of real rugby front row proportions, with an impressive tackle to boot.

We do the gig to a delightfully noisy crowd, which was a personal relief, knowing that Mike is in the audience. You don't want to die on your arse in front of your new fella.

Katrina and I return to the tiny stage-side dressing room, and open the door to find recently arrived Achilles filling up more than half of the space. It makes sense for me to vacate the room, take the gear down, meet Mike, let Katrina take off her make-up, then say a quick hello and head off into the moonlight for a night of passion.

Mike dutifully waits as I pack up the keyboard in record time, and presses a very welcome drink into my hand. We chat in the rear garden for a few moments, and head to the dressing room for our appointment with Katrina. I knock on the door, and Katrina opens it just far enough to get her head through the gap, her eyes wide as a rabbit in the headlights, sending a message that she confirms with the words

It's not convenient.

I know what you are thinking and you ought to be ashamed of yourself.

The truth is that Achilles was tying up.

A stripper, before they go on stage, must 'prepare' themselves to encourage the maximum size of their equipment, which usually means a quick gander at a porn mag, pre-packed and tucked in between the towel and the baby oil in the travel bag. The engorged organ is then 'tied off' – by an elastic band, rubber ring or shoelace – to keep the hot-blooded man as hot as he has to be. Timing is vital, as too long a tie can result in something resembling a black pudding, and not even a meat-eater wants to go there.

Picture the scene…

Katrina is on one side of the room, looking in the mirror, gently removing her make-up with a drop of *Clarins* and a cotton wool pad. Suddenly she is aware of a sound behind her, a sound clear enough to be audible over the pumping Kylie megamix that is pounding outside the door. It is the sound of slapping. Achilles is preparing himself.

I know some less principled people would have turned around and offered a hand, amongst other things, and many a drag queen of my acquaintance would not have hesitated before kneeling down and giving thanks to our Lord.

But Katrina was a good, if lapsed, Catholic girl, and steeled herself in the face of such temptation by thinking *I have finished work. He is getting ready for work. We are both professionals.*

I did notice that she had taken her make-up off particularly thoroughly before she came out of the dressing room that night.

Within a fortnight, I had fallen hopelessly in love, and it was time to hit the Pride party with someone holding my hand and my heart. It was still a working day, so I arranged to meet Mike at the entrance to the artists' enclosure at the back of the cavernous Tea Tent that Savage had demanded to host the insanity.

All the family were there. Lily, looking for all the world like Penelope Pitstop, Regina regally sucking her *Carlsberg* through a straw so as not to wreck the lippy, Adrella in a red military coat complete with busby, Tillie in a pink Marie Antoinette gown, Dave Lynn, Millie, Paul Adams, Tzarday and the ever-patient Murphy, trying to keep some semblance of order amongst the high-spirited and overly-excited collective.

I smuggled Mike into this madness, watching with a smile as he took in this carnival of queens, such a far cry from the suited boardrooms of bankers to which he was accustomed. I directed him to a spot by the barriers at the front of the huge crowd, where he could see the show, and – more importantly – where I could see him.

The noise inside the tent was deafening. It was a day where you could do no wrong, and each act gave the audience exactly what they wanted, with a chance to scream, shout, sing along and celebrate this wonderful day.

Katrina and I led the tent in a lusty round of community singing, culminating with our now standard finale *Puppy Love*, almost inaudible due to the level of screaming, and highlighted by Savage invading the stage, throwing knickers at us both before collapsing at the side in mock hysteria. We then joined forces and took the show home with our Edinburgh closer *These Boots Are Made For Walking.*

I don't know what had possessed me that morning, but I had decided that my outfit for the day would be a pair of white *Boy* cycle shorts, a white denim jacket, *Doctor Martens* and a winning smile. And I don't know what else possessed me halfway through this number. Maybe it was the heat, maybe it was the day. Maybe, and most probably, it was the confidence that comes for knowing that someone out there likes you, you like them, it is all new and exciting and it feels something like love.

But, for no rhyme or reason, I decided to seductively strip out of my jacket and let it fall to the floor.

Now, you must bear in mind that this audience of gay men had thus far been entertained – albeit brilliantly – by a procession of men in dresses, so a little bit of bare flesh was going to go a long way, and encourage a big enough response to almost rip the roof off the tent.

If the looks on the faces of Lily and Katrina weren't enough, you should have seen Mike. I couldn't tell if it was shock, disbelief, delight, or maybe a little pride and I didn't really care.

I was in love.

From luxury to heartache

July 15. My thirtieth birthday.

Katrina and a mutual friend Martin came over to my flat for birthday tea, cake and ice-cream. We had all known each other since drama school days and the room was every bit as noisy as you would expect from three theatricals, so when the phone rang, with Mike confirming our dinner reservation at Roy's Restaurant on St Martin's Lane, both Katrina and Martin *aaaah'd* and *ooooh'd*, in a good-natured tease at the bluebirds of happiness flying around my head.

Thirty minutes later, the phone rang again. It was Mike.

Hello. I'm really sorry, I have to cancel this evening. I've just found out my sister's been killed.
I gasped. Mike continued.
I have to go. I'll call you later. Bye.

I put down the phone, headed straight into the kitchen, and Katrina – knowing that something was wrong – came in to join me.

Pacing the floor, breathing heavily, unable to comprehend what I had just heard, I started to gabble about what had happened, how appalling it was, how she had a young child…

What do I do? What can I do? What do I say? Help me.

The party was clearly and absolutely over. Katrina offered to take Martin home and then come back to mine.

She later told me that, as she was driving, she told Martin of an article she had seen on the midday news... *I've got this awful feeling.*

My initial assumption was the death was an accident, probably involving a car, but by the time Katrina returned to my flat, I had been told the truth.

She had been murdered.

It was the leading story on the *BBC* evening news. We sat on the bed, listening in disbelief to the horrific account of a beautiful young woman, who had been viciously attacked, assaulted and killed. My heart was pounding. I felt sick. My mind was racing. All I could think about was Mike.

The phone rang. It was one of Mike's friends I had met outside the Gloucester, checking in, making sure that I was up to date with the appalling events of the day. He knew no more than I had just learned on the news, but promised to call if he heard any new developments.

It was getting late, and Katrina said her goodbyes and headed home, leaving me lying on the bed...waiting...

Just after 10, the phone rang again. It was Mike. He sounded extraordinarily calm, but exhausted. I listened as he told me of the moment he received the news. He spoke about his sister, already in the past tense, and wondered at the attention of the press on her youth and beauty, as if that made this dreadful act of murder somehow worse.

He told me that he was going to be out of immediate contact for a while, but would call when he could. I wished him well, and said all the things that one says in moments like these. Except there are no moments like these. I had no preparation, no rehearsed lines.

All I could send was my love.

As dawn broke, I went and bought the newspapers, and spent the morning reading every report, flipping TV channels, catching every update, so that Mike did not have to waste any precious phone time on the increasingly graphic and upsetting details. I just wanted to know about him.

In one paper there was a photograph of Mike, standing alone on a driveway, facing a wall of photographers. He was quoted as feeling *desolate*, and saying that *the true horror of what has happened has not sunk in yet* and my heart broke as I saw his private grief become public fodder.

With all this press attention, my mind began to brew a particular worry. Mike and I had been seen together in our local pub and out around town. I was a known face on the scene, and anyone on my arm would have been a source of some interest. It would only take one phone call from a mean-minded little queen to add an unwelcome but salacious dimension to this headline story.

That evening, I reluctantly prepared myself to go to work. We were booked to join Savage at the Vauxhall Tavern, which was the very last place in the world I wanted to be, but I hoped work might serve as some distraction.

Katrina had called Savage to let him know of the situation, and when I arrived in the dressing room, he greeted me with his traditional *Hiya, y'alright?* knowing that I was anything but. We didn't talk about it. There was nothing to say. No words of comfort or comedy were going to make anything better.

There is a rule in show business that no matter what is going on in your private life, you leave it offstage. No-one in the audience needs to know the whys and wherefores of your personal life. That's not what they have paid their money to see. If you get a kick out of watching other people's problems, stay at home and watch a soap opera.

I went through the motions of a performance, and no-one would have noticed a damn thing was wrong. But as Savage came on stage to join us, and pulled me up to the front of the stage, leading the pub in a raucous *Happy Birthday*, inside I could feel the lights going down.

Yesterday, everything had been so ridiculously right. I was successful, making good money, happily creative, and absolutely in love.

And now, I didn't know where I was.

But I knew I did not want to be here.

After a fortnight of separation and sporadic phone calls, Mike asked if he could come over for 'a chat'. As he sat on the sofa, looking as if he could sleep for a month, he kindly but clearly explained that family commitments meant we were going to have to *put things on hold for a while*.

I heard myself agreeing, and promising to be wherever and whatever he needed me to be, but inside my heart was screaming *Please don't leave me!*

We kissed, hugged, and said goodbye. I lay down on the sofa, still warm from his body, and looked at a picture I had framed that someone had taken of us at Pride, barely a month ago. Him, so handsome in a vest, jeans and *Timberlands*; me, bare-chested, white cycle shorts and *DMs*. Holding each other, smiling, happy. I started to cry.

OK, stop. Don't you dare. Don't you dare hijack someone else's grief and make it your own. Don't you *dare*.

I put my feelings in a neat little box, tucked it deep in some recess in my soul and continued with the business of living and working.

I kept my promise to be wherever he wanted me to be, keeping both my distance and my heartbreak hidden. I saw him when he said, and we even stole a night out at the theatre to see *Kiss of the Spider Woman*. As I sat beside this man I so desperately and now silently loved, I prayed that he would listen to the closing song, and somehow magically apply this sentiment to us...

> *Someday we'll be free, I promise you we'll be free*
> *If not tomorrow then the day after that*
> *Or the day after that*
> *Or the day after that...*

The day after that... he didn't return my call.

And he never returned my call.

We never spoke or saw each other again.

The lights went down...and out.

Why must the show go on?

There are great swathes of the years that followed of which I have no memory.

I know that I buckled under the pent-up emotions of those dreadful months, and had to deal with almost overwhelming anxiety attacks for almost two years, My hormones went into revolt, which resulted in an outbreak of adult acne, unwelcome at the best of times and a downright disaster when you have to sit on stage every evening. I know that I went to work, and that we continued to be a leading light of the cabaret scene.

I know that…but I don't remember much of it.

I do recall two nights at the Bloomsbury Theatre, guesting alongside Savage and sharing the bill with the brilliant comedienne Caroline Aherne, with whom we had previously shared a giggly and smoke-filled dressing room before a show at the Tramshed in Woolwich.

She had created the wonderful character Sister Mary Immaculate, dressed in the full nun's habit and offering spiritual guidance to the room filled with sinners. Even in my depressed state, I remember standing in the wings, and hearing her deliver the following words of wisdom…

People are always saying to me, Sister Mary, does God only love Catholics? Well, that's not true. God loves Protestants and Jews and Anglicans. He loves them all. He PREFERS the Catholics. Who doesn't?

Thank you, Sister Mary, for making me smile. Maybe there is a God after all.

Another moment to treasure was performing on the main stage of Brighton Pride, and being introduced by the iconic Richard O'Brien, creator of *The Rocky Horror Show*, host of *The Crystal Maze*, and owner of the skinniest legs in the known universe.

For the man who wrote *The Rocky Horror Show* to come onstage after our set and announce to the crowd *Katrina and the Boy…they were alright, weren't they?* was like a divine blessing.

We were – once – booked to do a gig with Jo Brand, in some very sedate civic centre in Basingstoke. Note the word *once*, as none of us were ever invited back, as the following story should explain.

Backstage, Jo was as calm and relaxing as a school matron with a mug of *Horlicks*, and sat chatting with Katrina while I peeked through the curtains at the audience as they arrived and took their seats.

Elastic-waisted frocks, cardigans, blue rinses and crafty comb-overs. Not our usual punters, but a gig's a gig.

We opened the show, and realised within minutes that this was an audience who thought the word *ruddy* was a profanity. They were suitably confused by our attempts at humour, but nothing could have prepared them for the assault to come.

Jo hit the stage with the gloves off and went for the jugular.

The closing moments of her act were some of the most outrageously funny I have ever witnessed. She decided to love and leave the audience with a list of the various euphemisms women give to their periods. *Arsenal are playing at home today*, or *I've got the painters and decorators in*. As Katrina and I stood in the wings, clutching each other, wondering if Basingstoke A&E were on standby, she delivered the final denouement.

I like to say I've got a lot of blood gushing out of my cunt. Thank you and goodnight.

It doesn't get better than that.

One particular cherry on our cupcake was a two-week stint in Bristol in 1994, co-hosting a supposedly radical re-take on the classic TV quiz show *Mr and Mrs*, uninspiringly titled *The NEW Mr and Mrs Show*.

We were led to believe that we would be the 'naughty' element of the show, that we were to be as camp and playful as we were on stage. We arrived at the studios, walked onto the studio floor, saw the set suggesting a garden, complete with polystyrene trees and a gleaming white plastic gazebo, and I leaned into Katrina and whispered *Doesn't look very naughty to me.*

Never was truer word spoken in jest.

Somewhere between asking us to do the show and our arrival, the plans had been changed and the programme was now as safe and as dull as it had been in its original format.

Our leading man, the dashing and now de-mulleted Nino Firetto, did a wonderful job of making the inane questions sound... well, inane... while Katrina got in the occasional quip, and I sat at the keyboard, waiting to be involved in the rarer than rare musical questions. My sanity was saved by the very jolly wardrobe mistress, who decided that the three lunchtime shows would feature *boho chic* and for the two evening shows, it would be *scanty panties*.

We filmed fifty-two shows over two weeks, usually knocking out five shows a day, and in each commercial break, the make-up lady would pat another layer of powder onto my suffocating skin, until by the evening I felt like my face was covered with Plaster of Paris.

The sweetest moment of the whole shebang was when an elderly lady, – who'd just had her five minutes on the telly – grabbed my hand and said *This has been the greatest day of my life.* It's easy to be cynical, but she was so happy. I bet she wore out the video, bless her.

My personal treasure is a review, written by the caustic Victor Lewis-Smith in the Evening Standard, who described Katrina *as being reminiscent of Gazza in drag* and myself as a *leather queen.*

Well, if the chaps fit.

The Edinburgh gang made a whistle-stop return to Scotland, with two one-nighters in Glasgow and the original scene of the crime, staying in a wonderful guest house, where each room had a unique 'look', and which prompted us to imagine a similar establishment, with each room themed after a certain drag queen.

Savage plumped for a leopard print and leather emporium, while Regina would be accorded a glorious Russian stateroom, complete with samovar bubbling in the corner. Adrella's would be straight out of *Dynasty,* with some camouflage netting in the corner to capture any passing squaddie, while Lee and Jimmy's would be akin to a front room in Weatherfield, with two uncut moquette armchairs, antimacassars and a wireless.

As we worked down the list, we hit on the name of a very successful and talented but rather snooty queen, who thought and behaved as if he/she was above everyone else.

Quick as a flash, Savage sneered *Bare. A bed with no mattress. Maybe a fridge in the corner. No. Nothing. Nothing at all.*

Savage by name, savage by nature.

Back in town and we were invited to join him for his final show at the Tavern. It was clear that his career was about to take off into orbit, with an increasing number of television appearances and three-night runs in prestigious venues, but work is work and if you're free, you take it. Once more unto the Tavern, dear friends, once more...

He had just returned from an enormously successful visit to Australia, leaving the Tavern at a loss on a Thursday night and, instead of putting on another drag act to fill the slot, the management had kow-towed to the popular monster of karaoke. I had dropped in one night on my way home after a trip to the theatre, to see the once holy stage of this legendary venue now invaded by drunk punters, screeching their way through *Summer Nights* and strangling the life-blood out of *The Greatest Love of All.*

I sat at the bar, watching and listening, wishing I wasn't doing either, and caught the eye and raised eyebrow of the acerbic barman known to all as Catherine Heartburn. As he clocked my grimace at a particularly flat note, he leaned over the bar...

I am noted, nay famed, for the milk of human kindness that courses through my veins he purred, in his very posh Edinburgh accent, before pointing a bony finger towards the onstage offender, *but that should be shot.*

I replied *Whoever would have thought, karaoke at the Vauxhall Tavern?*

With a smile laced with lemons, he answered *My dear, what you must always remember is that karaoke is merely Japanese for making a cunt out of yourself.*

Back at the Tavern, and the house was rowdy. Scarily rowdy. Give 'em a red scarf and a hot pie and you could easily have been on the stands watching Charlton. Enthusiasm is great, but this was almost out of control. The evening was in the final furlong and had, almost literally, been a riot. Savage was on-stage, being his usual brilliant self, when some fool in the front row threw up an empty can and it hit Savage in the face.

I have never had a stiletto heel in the forehead, but I don't reckon it's pleasant. But what followed was even more brutal. Something in him snapped. All the years of relentlessly touring up and down the country, living off motorway service station food, changing in toilets, playing in dumps, dealing with shifty managers and drunk punters all boiled over and Savage let rip, the diatribe of bile spewing of his mouth like soup out of Linda Blair in *The Exorcist.*

It was funny. Very funny. Savage was nothing less than funny. But Katrina and I looked at each other in the dressing room, and she mouthed…*He's REALLY pissed.*

It was the end. The end of an era.

The pubs and clubs became less about drinking and cabaret and more about dancing and drugs, and I found myself having to 'dumb down' the set list, replacing the wordier numbers with what we termed *singy-songy songs*. One evening, while battling away at Central Station in Walthamstow, I heard a voice call out *Do a Spice Girls number*, and I knew that my days – and our days – were numbered.

In the February of 1999, on our way to a gig, I turned to Katrina and said *I can't do this anymore*, and – gently and kindly – she replied *Then we don't have to.*

We saw out the year, fulfilling our obligations, doing the gigs and, without any great announcement, gently closed the curtains.

Word of our parting of the ways inevitably got out, and at our last gig in a packed Queens Arms in Brighton, the manager got on stage with two huge bouquets of flowers and made a very lovely speech. The audience were in tears and Katrina was in tears as she sang the final song, *Dream A Little Dream Of Me...*

I looked out and remembered...
the Comedy Cafe...
the RVT...
the awards...
Pride...
Mike...
the highs, the lows, the in-betweens...

and felt happy that it was all over.

It had been both a dream and a nightmare.
It was time to wake up.

For all we know…

When shall we three meet again,
In thunder, lightening or in rain?

The next time that Katrina and the Boy performed alongside Lily Savage, now known throughout the land as Paul O'Grady, was in May 2003 at the funeral of Reginald Sutherland Bundy, known to her loyal subjects as Her Royal Highness, the Grand Duchess Regina Fong, last of the Romanovs, Empress of all the Russias and Queen of the Black Cap in Camden.

An evening with Regina Fong was like no other.

She would burst onto the stage, a flurry of flowing gown and flapping fan, to be greeted by her adoring public, who probably knew her act better than she did. From a mass bounce-along to the theme tune from *Skippy, the BUTCH kangaroo*, through weird and wonderful cut-and-paste composites of film and television dialogue, and concluding with a club-filling line dance to Helen Shapiro's *Tell Me What He Said*, it was audience participation on a grand and glorious scale.

Reg knew he was dying and had made it a clear as a cut-crystal glass what he wanted for his last shoo-rah.

Sir Ian McKellen, who was a huge fan of H.I.H, was to re-cite Tennyson's poem *Wake Me Early, Mother, For I Am To Be Queen Of The May*. Katrina and I were to reunite to perform the beautiful ballad *For All We Know*, and Paul O'Grady would deliver the eulogy.

I had not seen Paul for a few years, except on television, watching his unstoppable climb to the very top of the show business ladder. It had been weird watching him transform himself from a caustic drag queen into the housewives' sweetheart, charming the elasticated pants off the ladies who take tea. Much as I admired the skill of this transition, I missed Lily Savage. I missed the unsmiling acid-tongued bitch in boots who would *rip your head off and shit in your neck* if you got on her nerves, who was now interviewing celebrities and being ever so nice as they promoted their latest film, book, song or just themselves.

I missed 'the good old days'.

Katrina and I arrived early at the Golders Green Crematorium, and were hustled through the gathering crowd in order to soundcheck. We had rehearsed the number into the ground, determined not to make the slightest error on such an important day. As we completed one final run-through, Paul arrived, immaculately suited and booted, and greeted us as if we had only seen him last weekend. We stole a couple of moments to catch up on our lives, all of which had changed dramatically since our last meeting. I was now a secondary school drama teacher, Katrina was working for an estate agent, and Paul was an award-winning TV personality.

Funny how things turn out.

At the appointed hour, as the three of us nervously took our places on seats beside the altar, the doors opened and the faithful poured in, filling the pews in a matter of minutes.

All of Regina's protégés were there, the drag queens who had shared her stage and her show, though never the bottle of vodka she used to down over the course of the performance.

Lola Lasagne, Nicky Vixen, Titti La Camp, Millie Turner and Sandra all sat in the front row, out of drag and clearly distraught at the loss of a good friend and mentor.

As Ravel's *Pavane* played, the coffin was brought in, bearing an enormous crown of flowers and Regina's trademark fan, beautifully recreated with red roses.

In McKellen's absence, the priest read the poem, before Simon Le Vans, the resident DJ at the Vauxhall, opened the ceremony, welcomed the congregation, and introduced Katrina and The Boy.

We had played at too many funerals over the years, for friends and sometimes at the request of friends of the deceased, but this was different.

Reg was not only a mate and a fellow cabaret act, he was also a legend, and we wanted to do the very best for him.

> *For all we know, we may never meet again,*
> *Before you go make this moment sweet again*
> *We won't say goodnight until the last minute*
> *I'll hold out my hand, and my heart will be in it.*
> *For all we know, this may only be a dream*
> *We come and go like ripples on a stream*
> *So love me tonight, tomorrow was made for some*
> *Tomorrow may never come, for all we know.*

I introduced and closed the arrangement with one bar of the Fong finale anthem *Tell Me What He Said* and, as Katrina's voice filled the church, I looked out at the rows of weeping men, and felt the enormous weight of responsibility, not only to Reg, but to his friends.

We were saying goodbye, and you only get one chance at goodbye.

We ended the number, and Katrina blew a kiss towards the coffin. I bowed, and we returned to our seats as Paul stood up, walked to the microphone and said...

I was fine until you two started. I was fucking FINE! Look at me, I'm in fucking bits.

The chapel rocked with laughter. Savage was back.

Paul then delivered the finest and funniest eulogy I have ever heard. Stories of wild drunken escapades. A side-splitting tale of announcing a miracle to a bunch of nuns in Lourdes. Every memory was laced with laughs, with devilment, with beautiful observation and with a whole load of genuine love and affection. We roared with laughter, our tears of joy mixing with those of sorrow, and we all applauded as Paul finished his tribute in his own inimitable style, toasting his old friend, his sparring partner and his partner in crime with warmth and wit.

At the moment of committal, with the sound of sobbing accompanied by Jiminy Cricket singing *When You Wish Upon A Star*, the mood was broken – without warning and in typical Regina fashion – by her theme tune, a swinging brass-powered version of *My Heart Belongs To Daddy*.

As the coffin slipped behind the curtain, the whole congregation waved farewell, flapping their fingernails and screaming *JUNGLE RED!*

That's the way to go.

A few years later, Paul invited us to sing some songs at the memorial service for his beloved Brendan, in front of a

197

star-studded audience at a club just off Leicester Square. I have written the details of our performance and the tale of a notable encounter as a postscript to this chapter.

Amongst all the heartbreaking tributes paid on that day, the most poignant moment for me was Paul, backed by a Dixie jazz band, singing my old favourite from the *Star Bar* days, *You Got The Right Key, But You're Working In The Wrong Keyhole.*

I did not know until that day that it was also one of Brendan's favourites, and it must have taken a lot of bottle to do that number, and to do it with such panache in front of the cream of show business.

But Paul never knew the meaning of the word fear, and if he did, he never showed it. There was that growl, there was that arched leg on *keyhoooooooooole.*

Time had not withered him, not one damn bit.

A few weeks later, and I'm driving to a party with the lovely actor Tony Maudesley, who I'd met at the memorial and with whom I had just spent a jolly afternoon at the piano, singing Beatles songs.

Paul was calling Tony's mobile every five minutes, demanding to know where we were, and how long it was going to take us to get there. By the time we finally arrived, the party was starting to swing, and as the volume level rose, conversation did too. Rather than yell in each other's ears, we decamped to the garden, pulled up some chairs and breathed in the night air.

We reminisced, told old stories, remembered moments of madness. It was both special and possibly necessary to reflect on the past, put it all into perspective and shake our heads at all the mischief we made.

As it was a birthday, party, the time came for the cutting of the cake and that damn song. There was a piano in the house and Paul broke my cover and dragged me to the upright, and I duly hammered out the chords while the assembled company bellowed out their best wishes to the blushing host.

The guests descended on the cake like vultures, and Paul pulled up a chair next to the piano and rested his pint of cider in the snug, as if he was in a smoky pub back home in Birkenhead, that land of distant voices and still lives...

Come on, Ian, play us a tune.

These are always words of terror to any pianist. I know hundreds of songs, but I don't know what you know...

Oh, wait...let's go back to 1991.

I played the introduction and started to sing, just for Paul.

> *I've written a letter to the Social*
> *To ask them for some clothing grants....*

He exploded, almost choking on his bevvie, *Hell fire, how the fuck do you remember that?*

I continued with the song until the end, and he looked at me and said...

Jesus Christ, that takes me back.

Seeing as we were walking down memory lane, I played the opening bars of an old music hall song that I had seen him sing on his first professional video, filmed in the early Nineties at the Hackney Empire.

I played and he sang, just as we had done at the Brighton Festival, over a decade ago. No-one was really listening, and we weren't doing it for anyone but ourselves.

> *It's the same the whole world over*
> *It's the poor what gets the blame*
> *It's the rich what gets the pleasure*
> *Ain't it all a bleedin' shame.*

I wonder what he was thinking as he sang that song.

Maybe about how he had achieved fame and fortune beyond his wildest dreams.

Maybe how no-one could have predicted that Lily Savage, host of *Stars of the Future* in the Royal Vauxhall Tavern, would become Paul O'Grady MBE, star of stage and screen and one of the most popular entertainers in the country.

Or maybe he was missing the ones who weren't there.

And I wonder, if a deal was on the table, what he would take? Past or present.

A seat in the *Muppet Gallery* at the Royal Vauxhall Tavern, a pint of cider, and a lock-in with all the gang, or a chauffeur-driven ride to another swanky do, with an endless river of champagne and celebrity chit chat?

You can't have it all, you know.

You can't have it all.

Ta-ra, chuck

The day I met
Cilla Black

What's it all about?

Being a child of the Sixties, I have a lifetime of memories associated with Cilla Black. She taught me how to sing a rainbow, told me something was going to happen tonight, but mercifully never asked me my name or where I came from.

I once saw her in pantomime at the London Palladium as *Aladdin*, with Terry Scott as Widow Twankey, and was intrigued by the colour of her skin, which seemed as highly tinted as that infamous barnet of *huuur*.

She sang *If I Had A Hammer*, though what this had to do with the story of *Aladdin*, I will never know. But we hammered out a love between my brothers and my sisters all the same.

I'd heard some disparaging stories about our Cilla, including some rather questionable behaviour with cabin crew, and how the corridors of *LWT* would reverberate with her announcing in the most satanic tones, *I'm not 'appy, Bobby* if filming of a certain Saturday night dating show that day was not going to plan.

But, as Ms Midler says, *If you want to be treated like a diva, you gotta act like one!* and you don't survive for decades in show business without sometimes stamping your feet until you get what you want.

I played the piano in front of Cilla Black in 2005, at the sad celebration of the life of Brendan Murphy, Paul O'Grady's late manager and partner.

Brendan's death was a shock. Just when the dreadful carnage of the 90s seemed to be over, when the funerals of friends were almost a weekly occurrence… boom! I was even more shocked to receive a phone call from Katrina, asking on behalf of Paul if I would be ready, willing, and able to play two of Brendan's favourite songs from our set at a memorial service. Without a thought, I agreed.

We had been asked to play at too many funerals in the past, and while the task was never easy, this occasion promised to be particularly challenging because we loved Murphy so much, and we wanted whatever we did to be both perfect for him and comforting for Paul.

We duly arrived at the club in Leicester Square, and met Paul inside. I had not seen him for a few years, as he had been busy becoming the nation's teatime sweetheart and assembling a stellar company of friends from the world of the business of show. We chatted briefly, all of us silently acknowledging the task ahead, sound-checked, found a place to park ourselves, and waited for the doors to open.

In they come. So many faces from the old days at the Royal Vauxhall Tavern, the survivors of the scene now mixing with the stalwarts of the comedy circuit, a light sprinkling of celebrities, and – on the arm of Christopher Biggins – Cilla.

The celebration begins.
But a celebration it certainly is not.

Everyone who gets up to speak ends up in tears, the assembled company is in tears, and we have been asked to sing a comedy song, the rewrite of *I Am What I Am* that we had performed together at the Brighton Festival in 1991.

This does not bode well.

I whisper to Katrina behind my hand *Let's drop 'I Am'*.

True to form, she says *No. That's what we've been asked to do.*

Paul, ushers another tearful speaker off the stage, introduces us, and a gentle ripple of applause washes us towards what now feels like a place of execution. I sit at the piano, look out, and ten feet in front of me is Aladdin – I mean, Cilla – resplendent in a smart dress suit, her hair immaculately coiffured, with a bottle of *Veuve Clicquot* placed neatly beside her shapely ankle, the Queen of Saturday night television... staring straight at me.

And when you're stared at by Cilla, you know about it.
I could read her mind, the cue card in her head...

What's your name, where do you come from, and what the hell are you going to do to impress ME?

As I underscore the introduction to the song, my hands are flapping like the wings of a frightened bird. Thank God the opening of the song is staccato.

There are some reassuring titters from the audience, as Katrina paints the picture of a frustrated chorus member in an out of town production of *La Cage aux Folles*, and – there's no escaping it now – time to sing the first line...

We all hate this song...cos it's so long...and it's so boring...

Biggins laughs, in the way that only Biggins can.
Loudly!

Sick of every step...three weeks in rep...ten weeks of touring...

The room starts to breathe, as if to say, yes, it's OK, we can laugh at a memorial...

It's the one show that's been done to death in every city
One show where you guarantee your costume's pretty...

And yes, I see teeth...those famous teeth...

Look under our glitz, stretch marks and zits...

Now she's leaning on CB's shoulder, chortling with mirth...

That's why we all hate this song

and we're off and and rolling.
First song done, applause.
Second song, done, applause, bow, off and *breathe*.

In the mingling after the 'show', Paul introduces us to Cilla, and she is all charm and tipsy smiles. *I luvved it, and Brendan would have luvved it, well dun.*

The last time I saw Cilla was at a happier event organised by Paul, on the occasion of his 60th birthday.
 Once again, the room was filled with faces from the grimy past and the glamorous present, RVT regulars rubbing padded shoulders with the cast of *Corrie* and *Eastenders*, Brian May and Anita Dobson, Janet Street-Porter and Barbra Windsor and – of course – the guest of honour...Cilla.

There was only one chair in the entire room, a high bar-stool, upon which she sat, looking for all the world like a dusty waxwork, surveying the room with eyes like a raven, almost daring anyone to dream about approaching her. She looked frail, but immaculate, and clearly delighted to be with her dear pal and chucklebuddy who had been such a support to her after the death of her beloved Bobby.

We did not speak, but smiled at each other, though I am certain she did not remember me. Maybe she liked my jacket.

I learned a lot about Cilla in the days after her death from the many tributes paid on television and in the newspapers. Ain't that always the way?

Arthritis. Hard of hearing. Who knew?

We all know someone who has lost their health, their hearing, the love of their life, and if you have hit fifty and held onto all three, you are lucky lucky lucky. We each have our cross to bear, our private pain. But we mere mortals can walk into a room, an airport terminal, a restaurant, and no-one knows who we are.

Celebrity does not allow for the privilege of privacy. The downside of being famous is that you cannot decide the day you want to be recognised, or the day you don't, and you can bet the bottom dime of the dollar that the day you don't want to be recognised is the day when everybody wants a picture, an autograph, a piece of you.

I thought about that lady on the high bar-stool at the birthday party and wondered how many painkillers must have been coursing through her system. How all the chatter in the room must have distorted into a wall of noise, how seeing all the other partygoers with their husbands, wives, partners and friends must have reminded her that she would go home and sleep alone, and how, when she walked into the room, every single person knew who she was.

Frail. Frightened. But famous.

That morning, as I walked my daily walk around Greenwich Park, I listened to Cilla Black on my iPod, stepping inside love, surrounding myself with sorrow, listening to a *Liverpool Lullaby* about a mucky kid, and remembering those Saturday nights in the Seventies.

Saturday night...

When entertainment was an opening theme tune, a slash curtain, silly sketches, conveyor belts and cuddly toys, a closing song and a catchphrase that sent you to bed knowing that there was no school tomorrow, and that all was well with the world.

Bring me sunshine in your smile.

Life, it's the name of the game.

Ta'ra, everyone, ta'ra.

The girl done good.

Song on the sands

The day I met
Armistead Maupin

Once upon a time

I have a confession.

I have not read – nor have I any intention of reading – *Lord of the Rings*. In the same modus operandi that I apply to the works of Dickens, Austen, and Hardy, I've seen the movie and that will do for me.

Indeed, all the books that I should have read, from Homer to Hemingway, from Steinbeck to Salinger, all those classics that everybody claims they have read – even though more than half of them are lying – I hold up my hands and admit to never having even picked off the shelf.

I don't read as much as I should, or what I should, and I am duly ashamed.

As well as relying on film and TV adaptations, I have a whole host of excuses, ranging from the flat-out lie of *I don't have the time*, to the pathetic *I read when I'm on holiday*, which hopefully disguises the fact that I have picked up some feather-light froth at the airport which will not distract me for long from the serious business of looking at the inside of my eyelids.

I was regularly read to as a child, my father dutifully working his way through the very wholesome adventures of the *Swallows and Amazons*, just before I got to an age when a girl with the unfortunate name of Titty was a source of classroom hilarity.

I used to read by myself, poring over the *Ladybird* books, starting with the riveting adventures of *Peter and Jane*, before graduating to the potted accounts of history, where the British were always the best and utterly blameless, no matter what havoc they wreaked on their crusades, and despite their predilection for burning young French girls at the stake.

A regular read was the perennial Christmas gift of the *Blue Peter* annual. Alongside accounts of cleaning Nelson's Column, and instructions on how to construct the potential fire-hazard of the Advent Crown, there were tales of great unsung British heroes and heroines, ensuring that there is a whole generation who knows everything there is to know about Grace Darling and her bloody lifeboat.

I recall John Noakes, that loveable mop-topped fool, attending a ballet class, and informing readers that the experience was punishing enough to fly in the face of the popular opinion that ballet was – and I quote – *only for sissies*.

School libraries were packed with battered copies of acceptable fare, so it was all jolly romps with *The Famous Five*, high jinks with *Just William* and close scrapes with *Jennings and Darbyshire*, all of them peddling an apple-cheeked vision of England, smothered in a layer of mud and custard.

I did become a fully-fledged citizen of Narnia for a while, drew an enormous map of the mythical country, stuck it to my bedroom wall and took to checking the back of my wardrobe on a daily basis. But after *The Voyage of the Dawn Treader*, it was downhill all the way.

I have read The Bible from cover to cover and there are some cracking good stories in there. I am constantly mystified that so many people have used the contents of this book to inflict so much pain and misery on others over blood-soaked centuries, especially seeing as the word *love* appears 538 times.

My first love affair with a book was inspired by a *BBC* dramatisation of Charlotte Bronte's masterpiece, *Jane Eyre*. Sunday evening in the Seventies was the traditional slot for a costume drama – shunted in between a wildlife programme and *That's Life* – as a gentle respite from the dubious pleasure of a baboon baring his beetroot-coloured backside, or Esther Rantzen presenting a carrot that looked like male genitalia.

Over the course of eleven weeks, I was led through Jane's abusive childhood at the hands of her despicable benefactress and teachers, to her role as governess, and then watched her fall slowly but steadfastly in love with the dark, brooding and troubled Mr Rochester.

In the process, I was terrified out of my very wits by the late-night visitations of the lunatic Bertha, who escaped from her attic prison to make bloody mischief, and whose ghoulish laughter echoing round the corridors ensured that I slept huddled beneath the bedsheets for months.

I could read the abridged version in a day, settling down after breakfast, reading the opening line *There was no possibility of taking a walk that day* and by the end of the day, I was in the final furlong with *Reader, I married him.* I loved it.

Holidays abroad became another reason for a damn good read, and I recall reclining on a sun lounger reading *Roots* – another big TV hit of the day – horrified yet engrossed by the accounts of the brutality heaped upon Kunta Kinte, Miss Kizzy and Chicken George.

But by the mid-Seventies, music had become my lifeblood, and the weekly purchases of the four broadsheets became my only regular read. Song lyrics became my poetry, to be learned and recited, with particular lines written on the back of my folders, and the lives and thoughts of musicians became infinitely more interesting than some dull old story in a book.

It was at school that I learned to lie about what I had read. I am sure that *The Grapes of Wrath* is a wonderful book, but for

211

a teenage boy, raging with hormones and unable to concentrate on anything for more than a minute, it was a total non-starter. There were plenty of stomach-turning moments when my English teacher asked me to share my thoughts on a passage that I had not even glanced at, let alone read and inwardly digested.

I rediscovered reading in the late Eighties aboard the fifty-minute train journey to the theatre company headquarters in Basingstoke, wiling away the hours in the company of a book, usually an autobiography of a singer I admired, such as Judy Garland, Edith Piaf, or Billie Holiday.

It was around this time that I met 'The Deptford Set', a collective of comedians, musicians, performers, writers, designers and dreamers, all of a similar age with the same ambition, and buzzing around the unlikely hive of the Pepys Estate in Deptford.

Daubney Tower was a forbidding monolith of 24 floors, with long corridors reeking of marijuana and roast dinners. The flats were only accessible by a metal lift, in which you got to play the unsavoury game of 'dodge the piss', regularly supplied by a resident with the descriptive moniker of Unsteady Eddie.

Saturday night was the traditional gathering of the clan, with a fortifying supper of quiche and carbohydrate consumed before we headed on to the Albany Empire for the *Outdance*. For we south-east Londoners, too poor to battle over to Earls Court, or too scared to stand in the leather-clad darkness of the Coleherne, it was the best excuse to pour yourself into something snug and shake some serious dance floor bootie.

Whenever the conversation over the quiche turned to what books everyone was reading, I sought refuge by the kettle, throwing teabags into stained mugs as the assembled company waxed lyrical about the latest group obsession which was the *Tales of the City* series, set in San Francisco and written by her famous son, Armistead Maupin.

Have you got to the bit where Michael goes to the club?
Did you guess about Mrs Madrigal?
Mona gets on my nerves.
Oh, I LOVE Mona.
I bet Ian would fancy Brian. Ian?

Ian didn't know who the hell Brian was.

Sugar, anyone? was my only input to the conversation.

To put me out of misery, someone took pity on me and I was presented with my very own copy of *Tales of the City.*

For those out of the know, *Tales of the City,* published in 1978, is the first of a series of nine novels, originally serialised in regular instalments in the *San Francisco Chronicle.* The book focuses on the residents of a boarding house, 28 Barbary Lane, and encompasses a myriad of colourful characters, detailing how their lives intertwine in a fascinating series of extraordinary events and adventures.

Up they rose from the Bay.

Mary Ann and Michael 'Mouse' Tolliver, Mona and Brian, Dee Dee and Beauchamp, Edgar and Frannie, and the majestic, mysterious Anna Madrigal.

Because they were originally presented in serialised form, each chapter is short, concise, designed to fuel the fire of fascination in the developing plot, and reading the book became akin to having a box of chocolates in the house. You try to ration yourself to one chapter, but just as you are about to close the book, your eye glances onto the next page, you see the name of a character who hasn't appeared for a while, and you can't help yourself.

You have to know what they've been up to.
Before you know it, you are finishing the book...and it's 3am!

Those in the know have likened Maupin's artistry with that of Dickens, drawing parallels between their genius in creating extraordinarily vivid characters, linking them together with plot lines that, in the hands of a lesser writer, would appear clunky and implausible. But Maupin weaves such magic pathways between and around his characters that each twist and turn makes you gasp with delight, and only serves to increase your hunger for more.

I fell in love with the work, and I fell in love with the writer.

In the film *Shadowlands*, directed by Richard Attenborough, starring Anthony Hopkins as CS Lewis, the creator of the Narnia books, there is a particularly memorable line.

We read to know that we are not alone.

This applies perfectly to the work of Armistead Maupin.

I felt part of the Barbary Lane family. I cared about them and about what happened to them in the same way that I care about a friend. With each new adventure, each new chapter and episode, I found myself walking beside the characters, watching them strolling down the Castro, sharing the welcome joint left pinned to the door, riding the cable cars, laughing and crying with them, wishing them well...

214

I was not alone.

But, it's more than that.

Just as Hamlet, in his instructions to the players, states that the job of an actor is *to hold, as t'were, the mirror up to nature,* so it is also the job of an author, but the reader has a very particular and personal role in the process.

We cast the characters in the story. We dress and style them, giving them voices, facial expressions, gestures and mannerisms. We design the sets and compose the score, taking the black type on white page and infusing it with our colour schemes and soundtracks. We work alongside the writer, but it is our vision, our own special creation, and we become very protective of it.

When I sat in front of my television set to watch the first episode of *Tales of the City*, in 1994, there was a particularly high level of expectation, excitement, not a little dread, and inevitably initial disappointment.

That's not my Mary-Ann! I cried.
That's not my Mouse!
No way is that Brian!!

The cast in my head was right and this was all wrong, because I *knew* these people. They were my family and I loved them.

I got over it.
Though I still have a problem with the second Michael.

You're the top

Maybe the Moon, published in 1992, is a world away from Barbary Lane. It is the tale of an actress and former holder of the Guinness World Record for the world's shortest woman, who spent months wrapped in rubber 'playing' the part of *ET*, and of her attempts to 'comeback' in a business where *you can die of encouragement.*

It is an atypical Hollywood love story, a wry look at the mythology of the world of the movies and show business, and has been described as Maupin's most lavishly praised – yet least read – novel. Maybe the public just couldn't hitch up to the new wagon, but I loved it.

In 1993, Katrina and the Boy were probably at the peak of our powers. As well as our regular paid gigs, we were often asked – and were delighted – to appear at fundraisers and awareness-raising events for wonderful organisations, including Stonewall, who one day gave us a call.

Armistead Maupin was going to be reading selections from his new book, *Maybe the Moon*, along with favourite extracts from the *Tales of the City* series, at the Haymarket Theatre on Sunday, March 7, in a fundraising gala for Stonewall, and would we like to perform an onstage musical 'thank you' to the man himself?

So, let me get this as straight as I can.

You are asking a rinky-dink little cabaret act, who can just about get away with it in a gay pub to an audience of rather 'refreshed' punters, to stroll onto the stage of one of the oldest and most revered theatres in London, and sing a couple of numbers to Armistead bloody Maupin?

Yep, that's about the size of it.

OK, what are we going to play?

The first choice was easy. *Moon River* was the 'theme tune' of *Maybe the Moon*, sung regularly by Cadence Roth, the heroine of the novel. For the second song, we had a chat with Terry Andersen, Maupin's partner at the time, and he told us that we could not go wrong with a Cole Porter tune.

How could we say what we felt about this man in one song?

That's easy. *You're the Top.* Job done.

Actually, the job was only just beginning.
I cannot read music.

Despite having piano lessons since the age of seven, under the strict tutelage of the formidable Miss Stenning, it just never *clicked*. I certainly stared at the page, pretending I knew what those dots and lines meant, but I looked far harder at my teacher's fingers as she played the piece and memorised where they went.

Fortunately, I was blessed with a good 'ear' and I bluffed my way through lessons, grade examinations, concerts and competitions, even winning the Sutton Music Festival Pianoforte Solo at 9 years old, to my delight and my teacher's almost offensive surprise.

I am not the first piano player to make a living out of playing music without being able to read a note. Technology has enabled a whole generation of musicians to skip over those scales, avoid those arpeggios and cut to the chase, and – with the bonus of an automatic transpose button on my trusty

Yamaha keyboard – I could rapidly work out songs for our shows in keys that I knew well, using all those lovely white notes and staying away from all the nasty black ones.

That's all fine and dandy until you are required to play a proper grand piano on stage at the Haymarket, and *Moon River* must be played in the key of E flat, which has lots and lots of the nasty black notes.

I practised for hour upon hour, until my hands were cramped and my fingertips were sore. This was one gig I did not want to mess up.

On the morning of the show, I woke nervous, and spent the whole morning with my stomach churning and my heart thumping. We even did a lunchtime show at some hovel in Woolwich, and still I could not settle down. Nerves turned to terror as we headed into town and arrived at the stage door of the theatre.

We were led onto the stage, and I sat at the piano, looking out at the auditorium, all those plush red seats, the gilt decorations on the dress circle and balcony, the domed ceiling, this hallowed arena where I had sat so many times as an audience member, and which now looked back at me like a courtroom.

How the hell did I end up here?

We were shown to a dressing room, right at the top of the building. I was presented with a programme, and on the cover was a portrait of Armistead Maupin. A handsome, posed, pensive genius who, by this time, was most probably in the building.

Sitting in a dressing room, with performance time approaching, I had an inkling of what it must have been like for the Christians, waiting to be led out into the gladiatorial Coliseum, or – for those of you who have had the pleasure – sitting at the top table at a wedding and waiting for those dreaded words *Pray silence for the best man*. You are the entertainment, facing a firing squad of expectation, and in two hours there were going be 893 immaculately manicured thumbs poised to seal our fate.

While Katrina busied herself with her make-up, I smoked and paced, smoked and paced, smoked and paced. There is never a piano backstage on which to practice, and as the time ticked on, the keyboard in my mind all merged into one big blur.

Where the hell is E flat?
What does the middle pedal do?
Will the lid be up or down?
Will I be able to hear?
How does the song go again?
Is it time?

It's time.

We were escorted down the stairs to side of the stage, and met with the compere of the evening, Ruby Wax, who smiled, silently shook my hand and then we all stood together, like British people at a bus stop, silently ignoring each other.
 Ruby made her way onto the stage and, as the side curtain was drawn back, I caught a sight of the packed auditorium.

Oh God…

Ladies and gentlemen, will you please welcome to the stage… Katrina and the Boy!

We walk onstage, I settle at the piano, look across the stage and there, sitting on a red sofa, next to Ms Wax, is Armistead Maupin.

He is casually dressed in a sky-blue shirt, blue jeans, with his luxuriant sandy hair framing his friendly, almost cherubic face. He has no idea who we are, or why we are there, so Katrina informs him and the audience of our role in the evening, as I play a gentle underscore of the opening bars of *Moon River*. Or as gently as I can manage with fingers that are now more like lead piping. It honestly feels like I have never played this instrument before in my life. I feel like Sparky at Carnegie Hall, when his magic piano tartly states *Your time is up, I will no longer play for you.*

Here we go.

I can hear the nerves in Katrina's voice. She's a belter and this is a ballad. We are in dangerous waters, and we need to power each other on. Three lines down, and I give her a bit more on the piano, and she is settling into the song. The melody is contained within nine notes, so no great vocal acrobatics are required, but that's when you have to find the pictures in your mind, and tell the tale within the lyric. For me, the most poignant words are *Waiting round the bend, my Huckleberry friend*, which conjures up beautifully romantic images of the two drifters, Sawyer and Finn, punting their log raft down the Mississippi. I used this movie in my mind to get me through the big danger area of the instrumental solo and, for sixteen bars, I am not in the Haymarket Theatre in London. I am riding that river, off to see the world...

But, no time to linger. One song down, one to do, and we're into more familiar territory. Every time I hear or play a Cole Porter tune, I realise that I am in the presence of greatness. He created melodies that go all the right ways, and his lyrics are always so perfect and particular to the song. Katrina and I loved a 'list' song, and you can't get a wittier list than the one in *You're the Top*. We resisted the temptation to squeeze in one of the many parody lines written over the years by lesser lyricists, *You're the breasts of Venus, you're King Kong's penis...* we are in the theatre, darlings... and we swung our way to the end of the number, bowed to the audience, and then to the object of our admiration, and exited stage right.

Back in the dressing room, and I smoke and pace, smoke and pace, smoke and pace. Even though we had been onstage for less than ten minutes, you still have to 'come down'. All that adrenalin, all those nerves, all that absolute terror has to trickle out somehow, somewhere.

There's a knock on the door and in walks....Cole Porter!

Of course it wasn't, but it was Nickolas Grace, who had recently been playing the master himself in *A Swell Party* at the Vaudeville Theatre, though I remembered him best as Anthony B-B-B-Blanche in *Brideshead Revisted*, which was essential viewing in the early 80s. He was very kind and complimentary about our performance, which was rather like getting a blessing from the Pope.

We head down to the post-show reception party, and I remember how much I hate these events. Everyone standing around talking too much and laughing too loud, with their necks straining and revolving, surveying the room just in case they spy someone more interesting or important, even possibly useful, who they *must just go and say hello to*. But there are lots of smiles, the occasional *well done*, and hugs and kisses from the people we know, and I feel like a puppy, having his tummy tickled.

A representative of Stonewall ushers us over to meet Armistead Maupin. He is, of course, surrounded by the good, the great and the gay, all telling him – and rightly so – how wonderful he was, the evening had been.

We are introduced and, for the first time, I get to look into his eyes. Wow, those beautiful, kind, all-seeing eyes. I thought of the mind behind those eyes. The eyes that see the world, the mind that weaves a world within that world. He is talking with Katrina, and saying how much he enjoyed our contribution, and they are laughing and doing that thing that people do at these kind of things, and I say... absolutely nothing.

I smile, but I say absolutely nothing.

Why? Because I am *just the piano player*.

Even though nobody says this about me or to me, I say it to myself. Even though the act is called Katrina and The Boy, and is and always was an absolute democracy, I am 'just' *The Boy*. The piano player.

This is not unusual.
Think of the Carpenters, and you think of Karen.
Think of the Eurythmics, you think of Annie Lennox.

Richard Carpenter and Dave Stewart were the writers and the producers, but attention will always go to the singer.

It's the way it is, the way it works and I am fine with it.

I am also inherently rather shy and, at the risk of sounding daft, I really do not feel worthy to be breathing the same air as someone I admire so much, let alone say anything to them.

There it is, out in the open.

And that should have been it.

The day I met Armistead Maupin.
Over, done with, and never to be repeated.

The best of times

May 2009 and a message on my answerphone.

Hello darling, it's Ian McKellen. It's my 70th birthday, I'm taking some gay boys to see 'La Cage aux Folles' at the Playhouse Theatre, and I wondered if you would like to join us?

I think I could handle that.

I arrived outside the theatre at 7.00 pm, and saw the large crowd of guests. Gay boys? *Boys?* It looked more like *Grey* Pride to me! McKellen, strolling through the throng, kissing and introducing everyone to everyone, Michael Cashman, survey-ing the scene with his beautiful blue eyes, Simon Callow, who always looks like he is just about to announce a Bacchanalian orgy back at his place, and right at the centre of the assembled company, Armistead Maupin.

True to form, I stood on the periphery of the group.

I was no longer working in show business, and was now a humble secondary school drama teacher, so of no use or interest to anyone.

I smiled at the few people I did know, who were in deep conversations with people they *just had to go and say hello to*, and waited for the call to arms from the birthday boy. It was nearly showtime and, as we went into the theatre, I found myself walking beside *you know who*.

It seemed churlish not to say anything.

Hello, you won't remember me, but I played the piano at the 'Maybe the Moon' evening at the Haymarket Theatre.

I certainly do remember, he replied.

And I believed him.

We continued to chat as we went down the aisle to our seats. He introduced the man by his side, the tall, dark and very handsome Christopher, as his husband, which was the first time I had heard someone refer to their boyfriend, their partner, their *longtime companion* as their husband.

I like the term *husband.* I love the term *husband.*

And, one day, I want one.

McKellen had bought the front five rows of the stalls for his guests, so we all file in, in no particular order, and I find myself sitting in the centre of the front row, next to Armistead.

So, let's look at what we have here.

Ian McKellen's birthday party, at a performance of *La Cage aux Folles*, and I am sitting next to Armistead Maupin.

This is, without any doubt, the gayest moment of my life. It couldn't get any gayer than this!

The show begins, and the stage is filled with gaudily glamorous drag queens, all hips and lips, pouts and preens, announcing, rather redundantly, *We are what we are*. It is flashy and trashy, we all know every word, but this does not matter one jot.

The story of Albin and Georges, a gay couple who own and work at a nightclub in Saint Tropez, and whose world is rocked when Georges' son announces he is to marry the daughter of an ultra-conservative father, begins to unfold.

The score, by the legendary Jerry Herman, punctuates the tale with memorable top-tappers and good old-fashioned show tunes. We roll happily from the high kicking opening number to Albin's hymn to cosmetic armour in *A Little More Mascara*, and then to the swirling declaration of love *With Anne On My Arm*. It's all as sweet and gooey and fluffy as a tray of Turkish Delight.

I realise pretty quickly that I am sitting next to San Francisco's answer to Santa Claus. Armistead is shaking with laughter at the smallest of gags, his deep resonant chesty chuckle adding to the absolute jollity of each moment, sometimes leaning into me and making the occasional comment.

As previously stated, I am a total theatre fascist who insists on absolute silence around me. No talking, no whispering, no sweet paper rustling, *no no no!* But, hell, this is Armistead Maupin, and he can say anything he darn well likes!

He grabs my leg at points of particular hilarity, as if I will somehow keep him in his seat, and stop him from falling on the floor in a fit of unbridled mirth.

You grab away, lovely man, you just grab away.

As Act One nears its end, we hear the love song sung by Georges to Albin, the shamelessly romantic *Song On The Sands*.

The lyric recalls how they met, all those years ago, how they heard a song being played by *a fellow with a concertina*, with lyrics that were s*omething about sharing, something about always*, and how, as is the case with the finest of songs, whenever or wherever you hear them, you are transported back in time and in place, and you are, once again, *young and in love*.

I glanced to my left, and saw that Armistead was holding Christopher's hand, his head gently resting on his shoulder, with tears rolling down his cheeks.

I thought how I was sitting next to a man who had created one of the most wonderful bodies of work the literary world will ever know, who has written – with such power and eloquence – that love is spelt with the same four letters, no matter whom you choose to love.

Here was a living portrait of that love.

The war was over, the battle had been won, and inscribed inside every one of those tears were the words *I have found the man with whom I want to share the rest of my life, and every moment with him is the most precious moment I have known.*

It was, and it remains, one of the most beautiful images of love that I have ever seen.

After the show, there was a backstage party, with a big chocolate cake for the birthday boy. The champagne and the chat were flowing freely, Cashman sharing stories about some very salacious door-to-behind-the-door-canvassing experiences, while Callow was still hoping that the loin cloths were about to come out or off, and I decided that it was time to head home.

As I said goodbye to Armistead and Christopher, I told them that I had been to San Francisco twice that decade, and had visited all the sights of the city that I had read about in his books. I had walked the infamous Castro, eaten chowder in a sourdough bowl at Pier 39, driven down Nob Hill and heard the scandalous stories about Ms Lillie and Coit Tower. I had posed in a cell at Alcatraz, bought a chocolate-filled cable car at *Ghirardelli*, gazed at the fog from the dizzying heights of Twin Peaks, and roared with delight at the stage-engulfing hats at *Beach Blanket Babylon.*

I had even been to Russian Hill, in search of 28 Barbary Lane, but it wasn't there, and I remembered feeling like Douglas Grisham, the little lad in *Shadowlands*, climbing into the attic in the house of CS Lewis, opening the door of the wardrobe, feeling his way through the fur coats and beating on the wooden back panels, trying to escape from the real world and get to Narnia.

It doesn't really exist...not really...it's just make-believe.

But, 28 Barbary Lane *does* exist, and so do Mrs Madrigal, Mary Anne, Mouse, Mona and Brian. They live in ours heads and hearts, like friends you don't see so much anymore, who have moved away, who you fought with, who left you for someone else, or who have died and live on only in memory.

They live, and they always will.

As we parted, he gave me a big warm bear hug, kissed me and said *Well, the next time you are over, you let me know, and you must come and stay with us.*

And you know what? I absolutely believe he meant it.

Though the years race along,
I still think of our song on the sand.
And I still try and search for
the words I can barely remember.
Though the time tumbles by,
there is one thing that I am forever certain of.
I hear La da da da da da da Da da da da da da
And I'm young and in love.

Two soups

The days I met
Wood and Walters

Hello, honky tonks, how are you?

This will make you laugh is always a dangerous way to start a story. With laughter, as with love, one can never assume that there is any guarantee of success.

An occasional and now estranged lover of mine once told me that *assumption was the mother of all fuck ups*, which turned out to be amusingly true in his case. He told me he was a Major in the army, and I assumed he was telling me the truth. It turned out he was a Catholic priest, married with two children and a cocker spaniel called Rupert.

And Father, he hath sinned many times. Many many times.

I can laugh about it now, and I love to laugh.

The first gay character to ever make me laugh out loud was Charles Hawtrey in *Carry On Nurse*. Thin as a pipe cleaner, bespectacled, propped up in bed, wearing headphones and joyfully playing a piano concerto on his meal tray. While the characters sexuality was never stated, it was implied, and in the Sixties and Seventies, implication was all we had.

As a nation raised on pantomime, and thus accustomed to seeing men in frocks, the sight of *Morecambe and Wise*, *The Two Ronnies*, the superb Stanley Baxter and the bulldog-butch Les Dawson all dolled up in drag never raised eyebrows or provoked insults, only laughter.

It was only with the emergence of Larry Grayson and his cavalcade of chums, Slack Alice and the hopefully dubbed Everard, his camp catchphrases of *Shut that door!* and *Look at the muck in 'ere* that the audience were confronted by a homosexual who might actually have sex.

The comedian Dick Emery created Clarence, mincing down the street with a handbag and a hat as wide as his flares, greeting passers-by with *Hello, Honky Tonks, how are you?* before indulging in some below the belt innuendo. There were frequent references to queens, poofs and fairies, all delivered to howls of laughter from the studio audience.

The undisputed star of *Are You Being Served?* was John Inman as the pressed and prissy Mr Humphries, who was more than keen to announce *I'm free!* and drop everything to measure an inside leg. His entrances onto the shop floor became as lavish as Dolly Levi returning to the Harmonia Gardens, with costumes that would not look out of place at *Beach Blanket Babylon.*

While all these characters were brazenly effeminate and outspoken, they were strangely sexless. The audience were cosseted into believing that they all still lived with their mothers, and liked nothing more of an evening than a knitting pattern and a cup of cocoa, the idea of the unspeakable act lost in a haze of talcum powder and bibelots.

The characters may have been loved, but they were created as figures of fun, even ridicule, and the catchphrases became part of the playground vernacular to tease and torment.

Kenny Everett, the anarchic star of whichever radio station hadn't sacked him, brought his gay sensibilities to the screen, and while there were no 100% homosexual characters, there were more than enough stockings and suspenders to keep the pink flag flying.

In the light of this dearth of inspirational role models, I turned to the rising wave of comediennes who were steadily moving in and barging the bow-tied sexism of endless mother-in-law and fat wife jokes back to the clubs where they shouldn't have belonged.

Penelope Keith as Margo Leadbetter – the archetype suburban snob in *The Good Life* – gave me many caustic lines to quote and imitate, Alison Steadman as Beverley in the classic *Abigail's Party* provided me with a new party piece that I will still drag out to this day, and *French and Saunders* provided gay men with comic sketches that were both relevant and repeatable. But my favourites were two Northern gal pals, who took the game to a new and still untouchable level.

Ladies and gentlemen, will you welcome...
Wood and Walters.

Wood and Walters, written by Victoria Wood, and co-starring Julie Walters, ran for eight programmes in 1981. Wood herself says *some bits of it were good, some deadly,* and the best that can be said of the show is that it was a dry-run for the infinitely more successful *Victoria Wood, As Seen On TV.*

The director Geoff Posner says of Victoria Wood's writing *She manages to examine people talking and capture speech-patterns and subjects that are everyday, but hysterical at the same time... it's quite unique to hold a mirror up to ordinary life and make it so special.*

Victoria Wood, As Seen On TV was essential viewing for all, but especially for gay men, who revelled in the toy box of wonderful characters and the waterfall of memorable dialogue, as camp as it was witty.

As deeply irritating drama students, we amused ourselves re-enacting favourite sketches on the early morning train into college, delighted as the corners of nearby newspapers lowered when we stage-whispered *Next door's had sex again last night. I mean, I like a joke but that's twice this month.*

Oh, what fun we had.

Funny lady
The day I met Victoria Wood

I was lucky enough to have a briefer than brief encounter with Victoria Wood after the filming of the opening show of the second series of *As Seen On TV*.

A drama school pal had secured the tickets, and managed to blag some passes to the aftershow party. It was an amazing experience, watching the process of making a television programme, from the warm-up, performed by the lady herself, through the seamless procession of sketches presented on sets that covered the studio floor like a travelling fairground.

The grand finale was a new number called *Let's Do It*, performed for the first time. A small Dixie band was assembled, Ms Wood sat at the grand piano and the song began...

Freda and Barry sat one night...

You probably know it, and if you don't, search for it on YouTube. It is the funniest song she has ever written, its joyfully naughty and bizarre lyrics detailing a horny housewife trying to encourage her less than willing husband to indulge in some very acrobatic marital conjunctions. Once you have had an invitation to bend over backwards on a Hostess trolley, or spear an avocado on your lower portion, your dog-eared copy of *The Joy of Sex* can be filed or thrown away. The words tumbled out in an exhausting stream of hysterical consciousness, the band blew and banjoed behind her, and at the end of the song the applause was overwhelming. It was beyond brilliant.

But then, the word came from above.
They wanted her to do it again.

233

No problem for me, I could have listened to it all night.

Here we go, *take two*. She gets about three-quarters of the way through and makes a mistake. Apologies are made, re-set, *take three*.

And about the halfway mark, another slip.

Deep breath, a request that we try and laugh in the same places, and *take four*. This time, the song has barely got going and something goes wrong.

Victoria is not happy.

A quick conversation with the gallery and the decision is made to wrap up the recording and return tomorrow with fresh heart and rested brain.

In the bar afterwards, I spy her, doing the necessary chitchat with the powers that be, and making a very reluctant attempt at mingling. She is clearly uncomfortable and itching to get home, but as she passes me, I politely stop her and tell her how much I enjoyed the show, particularly the last song, and how I thought she'd nailed it on the first take.

She replied, quite wearily, *I did. They just made me do it again for a laugh.*

I produced my book of her scripts, the wonderfully titled *Up to you, Porky,* for her to sign, and told her that she had kept me sane through the recent Chekov project at drama school, where I had spent six weeks working on seventeen words, and had adopted a Mrs Overall walk to my characterisation to pass the hours.

After she returned my book, and headed home for a cup of Horlicks and a Gypsy Cream, I checked what she had written.

To Ian, with love, Victoria Wood. And fuck Chekov.

Brazen hussies, headless barbies
The day I met Julie Walters

While Victoria Wood was the undisputed comedy genius who wrote the flawless material that made us roar and roll about with laughter, it was often Julie Walters who stole the show.

From the velvet-toned Margery, the afternoon TV host, bricking up windows to prevent heat loss, to the insane lady in the shoe shop, snapping off heels to make them flatter, and the iconic Mrs Overall in the spoof soap *Acorn Antiques*, we were utterly spoilt for choice. What Pele could do with a football, Julie Walters could do with a tea tray. The performances were always superb and the two best friends were clearly having an absolute ball, sometimes barely able to make it through the sketch without corpsing.

Sometimes it takes just two words to get a laugh.

Stupid boy.
Fork handles.
You Plonker.
Two Soups.

If you haven't seen the sketch, get back to your browser, tap in the words *Two Soups*, sit back, and watch six minutes of comedy bliss. A couple in a restaurant are desperately trying to order lunch from the worst waitress in the world, and that's it in a spoonful.

But just watch Walters. The weaving walk, the fluorescent teeth, the head wobbling like a Weeble, the repeated *Ready to order, Sir?* the forgotten 'soup of the day', the unacknowledged spillage, and the glorious pay-off after the disgruntled diners leave. *No tip? Bastards.*

Genius.

In 1996, Katrina and The Boy were cast in a TV film, with the promising title of *Brazen Hussies.* We were cast as *the cabaret act from hell*, but we didn't take it personally.

Our job was to take two songs, *I'm In The Mood For Love* and *Fever,* and do them them as badly but as well as we could, which is a tougher job than it might sound. The great Les Dawson was a wonderful pianist and certainly learned how to use the instrument long before he leaned how to abuse it. We decided that the key – or rather the beat – for these songs should be the *bossa nova*, a rhythm which can reduce any masterpiece to last dance at a holiday camp. Katrina added some sauce to the stew by deciding to sing in a broad Glaswegian accent, and I pitched the songs just over the 'break' in her voice. It sounded horrendous, so our mission was accomplished.

I was more than a little excited when I learned we would be working alongside the lovely Julian Clary as the Man in the Moon and Robert 'Citizen Smith' Lindsay as the shady wheeler-dealer Billy Bowman.

But most thrilling of all was the leading lady...
Julie Walters.

As the sun rose on a blisteringly hot summer morning, we arrived at The Rivoli Ballrooms in Brockley, the only intact 1950s ballroom in England, famed for its original decor and interior fittings.

It is a big womb of a room, with red velvet flock wallpaper, chandeliers, glitter balls and oversized Chinese lanterns. The walls are lined with gilt picture-frame-style panels, decorated pilasters and scalloped-shaped lights. There are two bars, and some blissfully kitsch booths, all leather-upholstered and tabled, and it had been the set for *Private Dancer* by Tina Turner and *I Guess That's Why They Call It The Blues* by Elton John, so we were stepping in hallowed heel-prints.

Into costume, and Katrina is dressed like some demented Carmen Miranda wannabe, complete with fruit-studded bee-hive and an off-the-shoulder sequinned frock, while I am tucked into a gaudy Bolero shirt, with massive multi-layered sleeves, and then disguised beneath a *Gypsy Kings* wig, a Jason King moustache and a huge pair of sunglasses. My own mother would not have recognised me.

And so to soundcheck. The dancers arrive, dressed and ready to be put through their paces, as we are plugged in, levelled, and then we launch into the first number. Clearly the dancers have not been told that we are *supposed* to sound as awful as we did, and their beautiful faces melt into a mixture of horror and sheer disbelief. But gradually the penny dreadful drops, and they spin and sashay around the shiny maple floor as we desperately try not to laugh at ourselves.

Our musical horror story is pre-recorded, so that we can mime to the number while the actors are doing the dialogue. It is a very long, slow and tedious process, but now the next lambs to the slaughter have arrived...the extras.

You can't call them extras these days. Oh no, it's 'back-ground artists'. You may not get paid any more money, but at least you are an *artist*.

I'm delighted to admit that I have done extra work and I have fond memories of doing scenes that required no acting skill whatsoever.

I spent a very warm summer afternoon in a bathroom in Barnes with Martin Clunes, and he has the most enormous areolae I've ever seen.

I got very giggly with Cathy Burke when filming a scene in a hotel restaurant for *This Year's Love*, mainly because she constantly had a fag on the go under the table.

I spent an afternoon in the gentlemen's toilet in the Freemasons Hall in Holborn with Stephen Poliakoff, which was especially memorable as he had a small briefcase containing a box of plastic straws, which he constantly chewed. Even more noteworthy was the fact that his flies were undone throughout the filming, but none of his team of assistants told him. Maybe that was the channel for his inspiration.

I told him. We never worked together again after that.

Extras, or background artists, are a fascinating breed. Some of them have been doing it for years, and could rival a cabbie for tales about who they have met and stood behind. There is a real pecking order too, right down to the queue for the custard at lunch break. The long-timers greet each other like old soldiers, and stand in packs, looking and laughing at the slightly bewildered newbies. They know how to pace themselves through the day, when to break out a book, when to suffer in silence, and certainly when to complain.

The *Brazen Hussies* extras are called to the set, all dollied up in evening dress. Some have clearly been up since dawn, doing their hair and make-up for their starring role in the background. One woman, in her mid-fifties, is determined to make her presence felt and hopefully filmed. I watch her rehearse her walk down the stairway into the ballroom, and Meryl Streep has got nothing on this gal. She is *motivated*, from her top-knot right down to her kitten heels, as she looks intently around the room, but for whom? Only she knows, but she is giving it all she's got. Every rehearsal, she is *there*, in the moment, a real professional. In a break, I overhear her talking to someone she assumes is the director, but whom I fear is probably either the grip or the gaffer, and she is selling herself in no uncertain terms.

I'll do anything, she says, her Bette Davis eyes daring him to doubt her determination. *Shower scenes, lesbian scenes, full frontal...ANYTHING.* Having seen the finished film, I am sad to report that she didn't make the cut. Maybe next time, eh?

Hurrah! Here is Miss Julie, looking neat and petite in a fitted little black number, blonde hair swept up, and beaming a smile at everyone. Robert Lindsay, already in character, is easing his oily way amongst the dancers. Katrina and I are on the small stage area, ready to mime our way to the pre-recorded backing track. All is set for a rehearsal and off we roll.

I'm In The Mood For Love is played, so the dancers can get the rhythm and the camera crew can line up the shots. The ghastly sound comes booming through the speakers and, from behind my sunglasses I fix my gaze on Walters as she shimmies and sways with Lindsay.

Oh, please find it funny. It's meant to be funny.
PLEASE please please get it.

Rehearsal stops for a re-set. She is grinning that gorgeous smile I know so well from the television and chuckling away.

Yeah, she gets it.

Midday, and I take an opportunity to escape from what is now the Rivoli Sauna, and stand outside the venue, grabbing some fresh air on Brockley Road and treating the passers by to a quick gander at my outfit. The number of vans outside informs the locals that something is 'going on', but they are used to having their streets invaded by film crews and actors. Once you've had Tina Turner and Elton John, everything and everybody else is a disappointment.

Next to the ballroom is a bric-a-brac shop, with an assortment of curios in the window. Headless *Barbies*, faded boxes of *Mousetrap* and *Operation*, with most of the pieces missing, sad-looking teddy bears and chipped tea cups. The owner is taking in the air and the atmosphere around the ballroom. She spots me and sidles up for a natter. She's in her late seventies, but her hair is as black as a tarmac. She clearly uses hair dye daily instead of shampoo, and her face is a ghostly powdered white, with heavy black kohl ringing her eyes and a bright red *Betty Boo* bee-sting mouth to complete the rather startling effect. She looks like she should be in a silent movie.

She asks me what is going on and who I am, and then proceeds to tell me the history of the ballroom, which is clearly a favourite topic for Our Lady Of The Bric-a-Brac. She leans into me, conspiratorially, and says under her breath...

Do you know, the gays have it on a Saturday night?
I respond with a noncommittal *Really?*
Yes, she repeats, *the gays. Wednesday afternoon and Saturday night. I did not know that*, say I.
No, she says, sharply, *you wouldn't. You're not gay.*
I smile and say, gently, *Well, actually, I am.*
Quick as a flash, she's in. *No, you're not. I've lived in London all my life, and I know a gay when I see one, and you're not.*

I consider the option of grabbing the actor playing the head waiter, who has been giving me the *oh-be-joyful* all day, and providing her with a practical demonstration, but I let headless *Barbies* lie, and head back into the heat of the Rivoli.

The dancers have been dismissed and all focus is on a table scene between Walters and Lindsay. Actually, it is an under-the-table scene, as Lindsay's character decides that he needs to persuade the lady to agree to his terms by sliding under the tablecloth, and serving up an *amuse bouche* that is not on the menu. It was a real education to watch these two actors working, refining and perfecting the scene, without a hint of a huff or puff when asked to do it again and again and again and again...

As I watch from another table, out of view of the camera, I am aware that I am not alone. I glance round and see the cleaning lady, who has obviously done her rounds with the duster and is taking a break. Lank of hair and baggy of upper arm, she is held together by a rather ancient tabard. She takes my glance as a cue to start up a chat, totally ignorant to the fact that it is 'quiet on the set'.

Who's that? she asks, pointing at our leading lady.
Julie Walters, I mouth back.
Is she the star?
I nod, with a smile.
Never 'eard of her, she says, folding her arms and hitching up her boobs, *à la* Les Dawson.

Ah well, I thought, maybe Ms Walters as Serafina in *The Rose Tattoo* hadn't been reviewed in the *Brockley Herald*, but we'll let it go.

At that moment, the director calls a break, and Julie heads off the floor, right towards the table where Mrs Tabard and I are sitting.

As she comes nearer, she smiles, fans herself and mock wipes her brow, to acknowledge the oppressive heat of the lights, the day, and the temperature of the room.

Before I can say a word, Mrs T is in there first:

Keep it up, love.
Yes, I will, says Julie, all sweetness and light.

She passes the table and, without any concept of how a voice can carry, Mrs T says:

You see. Common as muck, just like the rest of us.

I like to think that it was inaudible, but I still close my eyes and pray *Oh God, please don't let her think she's with me.*

Within a few hours, the day is done, the floor manager calls a wrap and we are all thanked and allowed to go home. There's a mass exodus towards the wardrobe and make-up vans, as the background artists race to sign off and get on their merry way. Not wanting to get caught up in the rush, I take my time taking down the keyboard and folding up at the stand, the regular ritual of packing up the gear.

After about twenty minutes, I head to the vans to return the wig, the moustache, the glasses, the shirt, and to have the now very shiny terracotta-coloured oil slick of make-up wiped off my face. As I walk into the van, I am delighted to see that it is deserted, except for the two make-up assistants...

And Julie Walters.

I sit down in the neighbouring chair, and let the crew busy themselves with a heap of *Wet Wipes.*

Julie catches my eye in the mirror and says *That was a good day, wasn't it?*

It's better now, you lovely lady.

What shall I say? Shall I ask if we can do the Family Planning sketch? Or the one in the Turkish Bath? Shall I tell her how much I adored *Acorn Antiques*? Or *Prick up Your Ears*? Or how I had taken tea with the real Cynthia Payne in Edinburgh and that she was actually as dull as ditchwater, and that her performance in *Personal Services* had given Payne a personality?

None of these.

We chat about the ballroom and how wonderful it was to be working in a piece of history, and giggle about what a bugger it must be to clean all that flock wallpaper.

And she is as lovely as I hoped she would be.

What I don't tell her is that I've encountered three women today who could easily have been one on the roster of her comic creations. Real women, doing their jobs, living their lives, all of them beautifully and unconsciously funny and all of them a little bit Julie Walters.

After the final wipe, I get up, tell her what a pleasure it has been to meet her, and wish her a safe journey home.

Ah, bless you, sweetheart. I'm just so glad that it all went so well. Now, I can get home and watch my soaps.

I love that picture.

This funny woman, supremely gifted actress and ac-knowledged national treasure getting home, after a hard day 'at the office', kicking off her shoes and sliding on a pair of slippers, before rushing to get something to eat in time to curl up on the sofa, ready for the start of *Coronation Street...*

And I really hope that it was a big bowl of soup.

I remember you

The day I met
George Michael

Sometimes the clothes do not make the man

Unlike most 21st century men, be they gay or straight, I don't have a beard.

I had a beard in my mid-twenties and toyed with a goatee in my thirties, but once the brown faded to grey and I was presented with the options of embracing the silver fox, dyeing for life, or doing the daily shave, the razor won blades down.

I had made it through three years at drama school relatively unscathed, without having to have a radical hair cut or alter my appearance in the name of art. Indeed, I resolutely refused to remove my make-up for a scene study of *Mother Courage*, when every other male in the year group felt duty bound to stopping shaving and smiling, and walk around dressed head to foot in black, topped off with a fisherman cap in sulky tribute to Bertie Brecht.

By the time it got our final productions, the design team decided that it would be a hoot to get the director to insist that I grew a beard, with the unconvincing argument that it was *The Seagull* by Anton Chekov, and facial hair was clearly going to enhance my performance of the caddish ladykiller Trigorin, as if playing a ladykiller wasn't going to be challenge enough.

After weeks of razor withdrawal, and that horrible itching that nobody tells you about, I had sprouted a fairly decent hipster of a beard, which suited me far more than anyone – including myself – imagined, despite the occasional tufts of ginger. Be warned, you beard-wearers out there, those are the first ones to go grey!

I have just one memory of my pitiful performance in *The Seagull*. In Act Two, I had to ravish Irina, my ageing squeeze, and the director decided that this scene of unbridled lust should take place around and occasionally on a centre-stage table. On opening night, as I set about kissing her neck, running my hands clumsily over the previous uncharted territory of a woman's breasts, I heard two very recognisable laughs ring out from the darkened auditorium…

One was her boyfriend, and the other was mine.

And that, my dears, is acting.

Much to everyone's surprise, including my own, I kept the facial fur, trimming it down to the uber-trendy designer stubble popularised by the lads in *Miami Vice*, but – more relevantly to me – on the very handsome face of George Michael.

I was a Wham! fan from the get-go, buying every record on the day of release, learning the dance moves from every video and loving every second of being on the bandwagon one more time. After that glacial posturing of the New Romantics, it was fun to get out in the sunshine again.

With the global smash of *Careless Whisper* and the aching beauty of *A Different Corner*, it was clear that the days of Wham! were numbered, a suspicion confirmed by the announcement of a farewell concert at Wembley on the hottest day of the summer 1986.

I slept outside the stadium, along with other young guns and gals, to ensure a prime position to watch the final throes of the latest pop sensation, aided and abetted by Elton John, dressed inexplicably as Ronald McDonald, who accompanied George on a poignant rendition of *Candle In The Wind*, a song the young teenager from Bushey used to play while busking in the Underground. Who'd have thought, eh?

Two years later, I witnessed the memorable meeting of two still-closeted gay icons at *The Party*, the first AIDS awareness concert staged at Wembley Arena, when George was joined by his arch rival, Boy George, to duet on the Culture Club ballad *That's The Way*, a musical olive branch after so many years of bitching, and an opportunity to pay back – publicly – a fiver leant in happier times.

Around this time, I forged an unlikely alliance with a very straight wine bar named *Casablanca* in Lee, a few doors down from my student digs. I had stumbled in there for a drink one night, and noticed that there was a stand-up piano on a raised area that could work as a stage, with the stool occupied by a black mannequin wearing a straw hat, introduced to me by the very laddish owner of the establishment as 'Sam', which was as offensive at it sounds.

He informed me that Friday night was music night, featuring a regular collective of local musicians, and if I wanted to come in and play a few tunes, I would be more than welcome, and he'd even move the mannequin.

Quite what I was thinking when I opened my set with Stevie Wonder's *Love's In Need Of Love Today*, which George had sung at *The Party*, moving through some jazz standards before closing with Billie Holiday's defiant anthem *Ain't Nobody's Business*, all performed in full slap and tat to an audience of the local plumbers, builders, office workers and secretaries, I will never know.

An even greater mystery is that I managed to survive without being lynched, but not only did I get away with it, I got a warm round of applause, a table full of complimentary drinks and an open offer to return whenever I wanted.

Within weeks I was a regular at the bar, rapidly, almost touchingly adopted as 'the pet poof' by this most unlikely group of protectors. Woe betide any passing stranger to the bar who made a derisory comment about me within earshot of the guvnor or any of the punters, who would step up to the ignorant offender and growl *He may be a poof, but he's OUR poof.*

The most popular and talented performer on a Friday night was a former cult punk singer called John, who had worked under the stage name of Billy Karloff, the ever-present dark circles under his eyes drawing a visual parallel with the horror star Boris. We had got chatting on that first night, and became good mates, so good that I was soon invited to free hairdressing in the shop he and his wife owned, beneath their flat.

After a few visits, I had befriended the girls in the shop, and one of them suggested, insisted, forced me to have some blonde highlights put to go with that designer beard. *And how about having your ears pierced while we're about it?*

In for a penny, as they say.

I picked up a black suede fringed jacket from *Top Man*, and these really fierce silver tipped and backed black boots from *Johnson's* at the World's End of the Kings Road, just like the ones George Michael wore in the video for *Faith*.

Ah yes, *Faith*. Nobody saw that coming, did they?

Extra, extra, read all about it! Lead singer of slightly cheesy boy band releases killer album, packed from first to last note with classic songs, all self-penned, arranged and produced, and the world falls on its knees, opens its wallet and worships.

Hot on the heels of the album came the announcement of some concert dates at the cavernous Earl's Court, which I had only previously visited twice. to view the Royal Tournament, and to twiddle my thumbs watching Pink Floyd build that bloody wall, while bleating on about what a bad hand life had dealt these multi-millionaires.

George? Faith? In concert? I gotta go.

It had been a long time since I had dressed up for a gig, not since the early 80's days of Japan, a cosmetically enhanced quartet I had followed from their shameful beginnings through to their acceptance and eventual success on the blow-dried wave of the New Romantics.

For an evening with Japan, you started getting ready at 10 in the morning. Outfits had to be constructed, tried on, removed, adjusted, and finally selected. Make-up had to be applied, refined, wiped off, and then repainted to perfection. Getting to the venue in all your glamorous glory was a test of the steeliest will, as you stood in all your finery amongst the scowling commuters, making sure that you kept your gaze firmly ahead and above the eye level of any potential aggressor. Once you had arrived, you spent every minute before show-time as part of the peacock parade in the foyer, sucking in your cheeks for all you were worth and trying not to look as if you were looking at anyone, but hoping that they were all looking at you.

Ah, those were the days.

Pulling on my black *501s*, a white vest, the fringed jacket, the boots, trimming my stubble and hair-spraying my high-lights into rock-solid submission, adding a little cross to my gold hooped earring, before sealing the deal with the obligatory dark glasses, I thought I looked the nuts.

Actually, I looked like a knob.

Walking to the venue, I felt the eyes of onlookers on me and realised I had committed the deadly sin of imitation, of following fashion as opposed to finding my own style. I was a mannequin, a copycat, a look-a-like, dressed in a third-rate uniform, deservedly the object of derisory looks and ridicule. It was a hard lesson that had to be learned, and it was the last time that I ever cloned myself.

Star people

Faith took the world by storm, and when it came to the award season, it was pretty obvious that George Michael was not going to be going home empty-handed.

My Casablanca wine bar buddy John was a published songwriter, and invited me to the annual *Ivor Novello* awards, the annual backslap and binge held at the magnificent Dorchester Hotel, where the good, the great and the lucky hangers-on gather to celebrate themselves, each other and their art.

I felt like a gatecrasher at a society wedding, but I was damned if I was going to let anybody know. Out came the leather trousers, an almost floor-length coat, and the now obligatory *Johnson's* boots. I primped and preened myself to perfection, and looked for all the world like a member of a chart-topping pop group. As long as nobody asked anybody which one, I was going to be fine.

The room was packed with linen-draped tables, immaculately laid, with designer-draped pop stars, immaculately sprayed, clutching sparkling glasses of champagne, doing the pre-lunch mix-and-mingle dance as necks strained and heads turned to see who had just descended the staircase to join the party.

Ooh look, Lisa Stansfield.
Have you seen? Brian May.
Who's that? Bros? Who are they?

Everybody was checking everybody.

If you were there, you had to be somebody. If you aren't, then just pretend you are. It's all in the game.

The paparazzi, who had formed a surly reception committee outside, lining the red carpet leading to the doors of the hotel, now crept in through the sewers, and milled through the assembled throng, poking lenses in the assembled faces, their flashbulbs creating little white explosions that set the chandeliers twinkling.

Suddenly, all eyes and flashbulbs focused on the arrival of George Michael and his entourage. Casually dressed in a cowboy hat, leather jacket and jeans, he was escorted by his protective phalanx to a table, pursued by shouts of *George! George! Over here, George!* from the army of cameramen.

The hotel staff calmly but firmly restored some semblance of order to the room, sweeping the media back to the foyer, before the kitchen doors were opened and with precision and dignity, lunch was served, devoured and cleared away, making way for the highlight of the afternoon.

It was no surprise that *International Hit Of The Year* was awarded to George Michael for the song *Faith*. The record had been a global smash, and within a snappy 2 minutes and 48 seconds, redefined George Michael's status as an outstanding singer and songwriter.

 The accompanying video not only doubled the sales of *RayBans*, but also proved that even if you can't really play the guitar, if you shake your perfect little denim-clad bum and pull all the right shapes, nobody gives a damn.

His acceptance speech was short, and laced with the standard fare of gratitude to the musicians who had played on the record, to management and record companies, and to the people who bought the record. Thank you very much, clap clap clap, back to table, pass that bottle and relax.

If you've been there, you'll know.

You know you've got to do a speech, you prepare yourself, stay focused and sober, do the deed, then sit down, content and relieved that it is all over and make up for lost time by hitting the bottle…hard…which is all fine and dandy until some fool announces that the final trophy of the day, *The award for Songwriter Of The Year goes to George Michael.*

The room rises to applaud and the clearly surprised recipient of the award makes his way, noticeably unsteady and clutching a bottle of wine, back to the stage.

All eyes on you, George.

Well, I really wasn't expecting this, he says, smiling and slightly slurred, *and to be honest with you, I'm a bit pissed. So, I think I'd better just say thank you and sit down. Thank you.*

Cue the laughter, cue the applause, and cue a pack of hungry paparazzi, homing in like hungry wolves, all fully aware that a full-page picture of a half-cut pop star is what front covers are made of. This is an opportunity not to be missed. It is bedlam, as diners are barged out the way by the ravenous pack, lenses poised like bayonets, all heading towards their victim's table.

And he knows it's time to go.

He stands up, slightly bewildered and the worse for wine, and weaves a winding path between the maze of tables, trying to avoid all eye and physical contact with the masses of similarly inebriated folk, all anxious to congratulate him on his success, and maybe get an autograph.

They're out of luck. No autographs today. This is a man on a mission, to get the hell out of here.

He's heading my way and I have a programme on the table and a pen in my pocket. It's now or never. *Carpe diem*. As he approaches, I hear him saying *I gotta go, sorry, I gotta go.*

I hold my ground, we are face to face, and our eyes meet…

To this day I worry that he must have thought that he had stumbled in front of a very unflattering mirror in a *House Of Horror*, as this low-rent reflection, complete with his dodgy blonde highlights and designer stubble, held out a programme and pen and said *Please? Just one?*

Bless him, he signed…and then he left.

It was the very briefest of close encounters and I never met him again, but I wish I had.

I would have loved to met up, gone for a drink, had a laugh, compared record collections… I'd like to have been his friend.

But…he had to go.

I remember you

The last time I saw George Michael in concert was the last time I or anyone else will ever see George Michael in concert.

After his 'coming out' appearance at a Stonewall fundraiser at the Royal Albert Hall in 1999, and his triumphant return to touring in 2006, including the magnificent musical christening of the new Wembley Stadium in 2007, the *Symphonica* tour, which premiered in 2011 and concluded on October 12 2012 was a strangely self-effacing and sombre affair.

Less than half the set was composed by the greatest singer songwriter of his generation, with only a handful of songs that could be deemed to be genuine hits, but still the faithful gathered, filling every seat of Earls Court, an inappropriate setting for such an intimate show.

The audience were mostly the wrong side of forty, with the occasional thirty something and groovy granny thrown in, some clutching their bags of goodies – t-shirts, caps, keyrings, and coffee mugs – procured from the well-stocked merchandise stand.

There were a healthy gaggle of gays, the clutch of obsessives doing every date on the tour, and a few grumpy husbands dragged along by *the wife*, silently plotting of a night of marital revenge in the company of Iron Maiden.

As the house lights dimmed and the crowd roared expectantly, the sound of the orchestra swelled from behind the vibrant red curtain that enveloped the stage, filling the arena with the foreboding introduction to *Through*, the finale to the most recent album *Patience*, released a long eight years ago.

A starburst of lights, the plucked strings of a harp and then…that voice.

Is that enough? I think it's over.
See, everything has changed.
And all this hatred may just make me strong enough
To walk away.

Hardly a song or a sentiment to get the place up and rocking, but it became quickly apparent that this was not to be an evening of crowd-pleasing sing-a-longs.

Long gone were the *shuttlecock-down-the-shorts* days of Wham! and the hip-shaking scream machine of the *Faith* era.

Most of the set was performed seated on a silver barstool, with the suited and spectacled superstar wrapping his notice-ably deeper but no less divine tones around songs by New Order, Sting, Rhianna and Rufus Wainwright, with some jazz swingers and standards thrown into the intoxicating but almost overwhelmingly melancholic mix.

It was the last night of a long tour, and one which had been dramatically interrupted by a near-fatal brush with pneumonia and three-week residency in the intensive care unit of an Austrian hospital, and the emotion of this final furlong was evident as George expressed his heartfelt gratitude to the band, the orchestra, the crew and the audience.

The closing number was *I Remember You*, a song I first heard as a child, as it was hung, drawn and yodelled by Frank Ifield, but which had been radically revisited and refined on the much-maligned *Songs Of The Last Century* collection.

The song was sung in memory of his late partner Anselmo Feleppa, whose death had inspired the album *Older*. A musical love letter to the man who had opened up his heart and the possibility of life as a happy homosexual, and whose passing would signal the beginning of an extended mourning and a slow descent into a world of drug-fuelled dismay.

The beautiful arrangement of harp and voice allowed the emotional punch of every word to express the agony of lost love and of the only comfort to be found, buried deep in the treasure box of memory.

As he introduced this final curtain call as a lullaby, he made a hopeful request to the audience to *Try and restrain yourself from screaming*, which fell on some sadly unsympathetic ears, as random shouts of *I love you, George!* screeched out in the darkness.

Fortunately I was three rows from the stage, and therefore close enough to absolutely focus on the singer and the song.

And I remembered you. And you. And you.

As he sang the last line, he pointed his finger out at the audience and around the arena as the onstage cameras projected the standing ovation on the huge screen behind him, and for a fleeting moment I saw myself, smiling, applauding, standing right beside George Michael.

A bow, a wave…and he was gone.

Feels good to be free

On the morning after the day George Michael died, I thought of the lyrics to *Through*, that he had sung at that now final performance.

> *So hear me now, I've enough of these chains*
> *I know they're of my making*
> *No-one else to blame for where I stand*
> *Today, I've no memory of truth*
> *But suddenly the audience is so cruel*
> *So God, hey God, you know why I'm through.*

I also remembered the last words of the play-out song, as the star of the show disappeared backstage and the arena emptied *Feels good to be free.*

There had been many times over the years when I worried that George Micheal had not enjoyed his success for one single minute, that the very thing that had brought so much joy to so many millions had brought him little more than misery.

As he wrote in *Waiting*, the closing track of *Listen Without Prejudice*, that furrow-browed hangover after the *Faith* party, which had seen all his dreams of fame and fortune exceed his wildest expectations, but had also brought him a whole trunk of loneliness and paranoia *You look for your dreams in heaven, but what the hell are you supposed to do when they come true?*

I had watched in desperation as I witnessed his self-destruction, the desperate pursuit of drug-induced euphoria or the fleeting gratification of anonymous sex, which I found so hard to associate with the man who held such a fierce grip of control and perfectionism over his public persona and his professional output.

Every report that rejoiced in his many and varied indiscretions seemed totally at odds with a man who could touch the heart, move the feet, and hold Wembley Stadium in the palm of his hand and elicit as great an outpouring of joyful affection and admiration from an audience as I have ever seen.

And while it wasn't my place to worry, I was certainly more than a little concerned because I loved him, as stupid as that may sound, as you can love a man you only know from his music. I did, I do, and I always will.

On that cold and misty Boxing Day morning, I listened to his final single release, the distressingly poignant *White Light*, where he pays tribute to stars that have shone so brightly and burned out before their time, and one line in particular seared out of the speakers and into my heart.

Maybe he just wanted to be free.

George Michael sang a lot about freedom, how he didn't want *your* freedom, that you've got to *give for what you get…* and now he is free. Free from the pressure to produce the next hit song, to go out on the road and sell sell sell, free from the demands of the public and the press, free from being scrutinised both on and off stage, free from being George Michael, free to be Georgios Kyriacos Panayiotou.

Sometimes it's easier to be someone other than yourself.

You can adopt a stage name, grow a beard, bleach your hair, hide behind a pair of dark glasses, only show and tell people as much as they need to know, and play the version of yourself with which you are most comfortable, maybe the one that hides all the things you dislike about yourself and would really like to change.

I did that. Sometimes I think I still do.

But what do you do when that version of yourself makes you a world-wide superstar, and every dream you ever had comes true?

When you fear that making the slightest change, revealing the most minute flaw, or the discovery of hidden truth about yourself will make everyone turn their back on you, and then where will you be?

You will be all alone, with a wardrobe of clothes that just don't fit anymore, a beard that is starting to grey, a pair of dark glasses you wear to keep the world away, and a dream that became a nightmare.
You will eventually have to face yourself, and decide which version of yourself was really worth your while, which one will really set you free and let you be happy.

We can create, polish and present an image of ourselves, strapped on like a suit of armour, but we don't recognise the weight of the damn thing until the war is over, we step away from the battlefield, and find our own particular and personal peace.

I hope that Georgios Panayiotou has found that peace.

If there is a heaven, I hope that he is reunited with Anselmo, and that they will walk on the beach, play with their dogs, swim in the ocean and love each other beyond time and eternity.

That will be enough.

Sleep well, George.

The wizard and I

The day I met
Ian McKellen

Clause and effect

Once upon a not too long ago, in this land where we live, there ruled a wicked witch called Margaret. Although she was born the daughter of a humble greengrocer, she always dreamed of a day when she would rule over all, and everybody would believe that what she thought and what she said was absolutely right.

She snatched milk from the mouths of innocent school children, clawed her way to power and embarked on her plan to rule the land with discord, error, doubt and despair. She stole from the poor and gave to the rich, destroyed industries and communities, led the country to war and inflicted irreparable damage on the lives of millions.

She was a very wicked witch indeed.

At this time, there was a belief held by most of the court that the love shared between two people of the same sex was wrong. Not different, not even unusual, but wrong.

Despite the sterling work of the Guiding Light Council, led by Count Ken of Livingstone – who not only passionately supported this right to love, but also provided many points of refuge for these much put-upon people – there was a concerted effort to make sure that this view remained not only unchallenged, but condoned.

Schools across the land were advised not to include reference to these outcasts and their practices, to protect children from this evil.

When a book entitled *Jenny lives with Eric and Martin* was unearthed in a school library by a spy, concealed in his daily chain mail, the court rose up in rage and battle lines were drawn between those who believed that children should be able to read and learn about anything and everything, and those who believed that there are some things that should be kept hidden away, for fear it might confuse, influence and pervert.

The Wicked Witch summoned a dumpy troll, known to her supporters as Jill, the Dark Knight, to sally forth and demonise this book and all others that dared to suggest that love is love is love, always spelt with the same four letters. She railed about how these books showed children of five and six all about homosexuality and how it was done, with explicit descriptions of intercourse. She claimed that the books glorified homosexuality, and actively encouraged youngsters to believe that it was indeed better than any other sexual way of life.

The cadaverous Lord of Somers added his little drops of poison to the brew, citing the animal kingdom to show that this lifestyle was abnormal, and likened learning about homosexuality as akin to picking up a bad habit. Finally, the Wicked Witch demanded that children needed to be taught to respect traditional moral values, and not that they had *an inalienable right to be gay.*

Fortunately, not all the courtiers agreed.

The noble Wedgewood-Benn warned the court that aligning the word *promote* with the word *describe* would make the ludicrous implication that every murder play promotes murder, that every war play promotes war, and that every drama involving the eternal triangle promotes adultery. But his words fell on deaf and stupid ears and the motion to prevent the promotion of love between two members of the same sex as a normal way of life was carried and became law.

And thus Clause 28 of the Local Government Bill was born.

I know, it sounds like a fairy tale.

In this day and age – with civil partnerships, same sex marriages, and members of the LGBT community acknowledged, admired, and rewarded for their contribution to the world – it seems hard to believe that a little over a quarter of a century ago, this absurd school of thought even existed.

We had fought hard and long to drag the image of homosexuality out of the public toilets, away from the spectre of dirty old men prowling the parks. We had shredded the unwarranted labels of paedophiles and perverts, and come out as proud, liberated and loving members of society, and it really had seemed that genuine progress had been made.

The advent of HIV/AIDS, and the knee-jerk apportion of blame hurled at the gay community, rapidly undid all the good that had been done. Storm clouds of God-coated fascism rained down on our parade, and the disease was deemed a heavenly judgement, divine retribution upon our wicked and promiscuous world.

But, when the going gets tough…

We were no longer prepared to see our march of progress halted and pushed back. It was time to come out loud and come out fighting.

It was no longer enough to sit in bars or around dinner tables and *tut-tut* away, knocking back the Chardonnay while listening to show tunes and thinking that there was nothing that we could do, or should do, to change the world. We could, and we should, and the time was now.

At 6pm on May 23 1988, the night before Clause 28 became law as Section 28, the *BBC* newsroom was invaded by a group of lesbians, chanting against the Clause, with one game girl managing to chain herself to the chair of the previously unflappable Sue Lawley, whilst another had the dubious pleasure of being sat upon by Nicholas Witchell, which – as far as I know – did not convert her from her chosen lifestyle.

The fight back had begun.

Deeds not words, declared Emmeline Pankhurst, as she marshalled her army of Suffragettes at the turn of the century, when all peaceful efforts to win the vote for women had failed.

Deeds *and* words became the clarion call behind the evening entitled *Before The Act*, that was staged at the Piccadilly Theatre on June 5 1988.

The day I met Ian McKellen.

Before the act

I was invited by Wendy and Trina, coordinators of the evening, to 'help out' backstage at this evening, working as a runner on what promised to be a night that would be remembered not only for its fists-up defiance, but also for the gathering of stars that would stand together and expose this law as a dangerous and offensive invasion into the classroom.

Every piece of work to be presented was the creation of a gay man or lesbian, with the inference that once you start banning literature that even remotely promotes homosexuality, purely by the virtue that it was written by a gay man or lesbian, where do you stop? Do you prohibit the music of Bernstein and Tchaikovsky? Do you ban the plays of Coward, Williams and Orton? How many authors, poets, painters, sculptors, songwriters and composers must be consigned to a moralistic dustbin just in case someone might see or hear something that dares to suggest that being gay is not only normal, but good?

I arrived at the Piccadilly as dawn was breaking and the early morning hum of London traffic was echoing around the streets, and walked through the stage door into that magical world of barely-organised chaos, excitement, nerves and expectation that exists backstage when a show is being put together on that day to be presented that night.

As the morning wore on, I sneaked into the auditorium to watch the rehearsals. On stage were Sheila Hancock, with her beloved partner John Thaw, and Gary Oldman, rehearsing a scene from Orton's *Entertaining Mister Sloane*. I had fallen in love with Ms Hancock when I first saw her working alongside Richard Briers in an early Seventies production of Alan

Ayckbourn's *Absurd Person Singular*, when her performance as a suburban housewife trying to commit suicide at a Christmas party was one of the funniest things I had seen in my young life.

She had lost none of her comic skills, and I stood in the dress circle, stifling my giggles as she revelled in the glorious line *I'm all in the rude under this dress.* Later as I wandered into the huge communal dressing room, I actually got to see under her dress – there she was, with her hubby, finding a corner to call their own and stripped unashamedly down to their smalls. No dressing room, no airs and graces, looking for all the world like a couple getting changed on the beach.

Despite the stellar gathering of the very cream of the acting profession, I was most excited by the presence of the Pet Shop Boys, and was more than delighted to be put in charge of caring for the needs of the dynamic duo. This show was to be their first live appearance, and their arrival sent a buzz around the theatre.

I settled into the auditorium to listen to the soundcheck, watching as an arsenal of equipment arrived and was slowly, very slowly assembled by a group of roadies. The day had been rapid succession of act after act, scene after scene, a speedy conveyor belt of quick lighting checks, cues, intros and exits, and onto the next item. Now everything ground to a halt.

As I sat, watching the stage being filled with keyboards, monitors, speakers and miles of cable, I was aware of a very famous figure taking in the proceedings.

Ian McKellen, one of the organisers of the event, was quietly but clearly concerned with the halt in the running of the day. He had recently appeared in the Pet Shop Boys video for *Heart*, playing a blood-hungry vampire, and had used the connection to invite the hottest pop group of the day to take part in this historic evening. But his special guests were throwing a right royal spanner in the works, and time was ticking on and away.

He prowled the aisles, nervously biting his lip, unable to do anything but wait for the necessary doings to be done. He saw me, smiled, and walked over, and sat down next to me.

What do I say?
Loved your Coriolanus. No, maybe not.

Fortunately, he spoke first.
I thought they were just going to do a couple of songs with a piano.

I chuckled inside and remarked that, while that would certainly have been easier, that would not be the Pet Shop Boys. He smiled, nodded, and wandered back to the front of the stage to try to hustle things along.

Eventually, the equipment was set, the sound was checked and I escorted them to their dressing room, with Neil Tennant behind walking in stately silence, while Chris Lowe jabbered away to me, ten to the dozen, in an intriguing reversal of their onstage personas. It's always the quiet ones you have to look out for.

As the clock ticked towards showtime, every corridor was crammed with the good, the great and the legendary.

Rupert Everett was in loud and high spirits, making his effervescent presence known to all, while the dark brooding figure of Anthony Sher stood silently in a corner, like a passenger on a crowded train who just wanted to get off and get home. Faces I knew but couldn't name arrived in droves, until the 300 strong cast of the evening were assembled backstage and the house filled with those lucky enough to secure a ticket for this unique evening of theatre, music, history and protest.

In olden days a glimpse of stocking
was looked on as something shocking
Now, heaven knows, anything goes.

Except it wouldn't, if Section 28 was enforced.

Now – according to this new law – the sight of two pairs of socks on a bedroom floor could turn a child homosexual. Reading books, listening to music, watching plays and films, anything that presented a gay lifestyle as 'normal' was up for scrutiny and prohibition.

As the rich artistic feast of the evening continued, the message was underlined with every word spoken and every note played and sung. If you remove this work, you cheat the world by burying priceless treasures and locking life and love behind a door of bigotry and blinkered morality.

Each performer was greeted and applauded with warmth and appreciation. Stephen Fry and Alan Bennett won particularly loud rounds of applause for stepping out on stage and coming out of the closet. Simon Rattle conducted works by Britten and Poulenc. The Pet Shop Boys acquitted themselves admirably with a set which included the poignant *It Couldn't Happen Here.* The regal Joan Plowright was magnificent as *A Woman of No Importance* and Mckellen was masterful in a powerful scene from Martin Sherman's groundbreaking play *Bent.*

The show concluded with a breathtaking assemblage of theatrical heavyweights: Vanessa Redgrave, Judi Dench, Harold Pinter, Miranda Richardson, Simon Callow, Alec

McCowen, Edna O'Brien, Paul Eddington, Alan Bates and Francesca Annis taking it in turns to read poetry by Marlowe, Williams, Housman, Duffy, Auden and Wilde.

As I stood in the wings, watching the best performers in the land presenting some of the best work in the world, I realised I was standing next to an elderly lady in a fur coat listening attentively to this extraordinary collective of men and women.

I was standing next to Dame Peggy Ashcroft.

As the show closed, and the entire cast came on to the stage and threw pink roses into the audience, I was aware that when the applause ended, the real battle had only just begun.

The next event was held at a small theatre in Hackney. I had proved myself to be a worthy runner and my services were requested to look after the main players; Ian McKellen, Michael Cashman, and the superb transgender magician, Faye Presto. I made countless cups of tea – whether they wanted them or not – and made sure all calls and props were prepared and ready to roll.

At the end of the evening, I was watching from the wings as the company sang an *en masse* rendition of *Over The Rainbow.* McKellen saw me, came over, put his arm round my shoulder and prompted me to venture onto the stage. *Oh, why not?* I thought. Then I can say that I've been onstage with the best in the business. Not too shoddy for someone fresh out of drama school.

Fresh out of drama school and living in a tiny box-room in a shared flat. There was just enough room for a bed, a cupboard, and my few belongings, piled on the floor, leaving a narrow pathway to the middle of the mattress. It was hardly glamorous, but it was a roof over my head at a very affordable rent.

One afternoon, the phone rang.

Hello, this is Ian McKellen. I got your number off the Vixens, and I was wondering if you are free next week and would like to accompany me to the Kirov Ballet?

I spluttered that I would be delighted.

Oh marvellous, he said. *We could meet at mine in the afternoon and then head over to Islington.*

I asked for directions to his home, and was gently informed that a car would be sent to collect me.

Cinderella, you shall go to the ball.

Well, we've got a few hours...

It's a strange moment when you ring an ordinary doorbell and an extraordinary man opens the door.

There stood Richard the Second...
Macbeth...
Salieri....
Ian McKellen.

And he was bald.

After the film *Scandal* – where he played the shamed sex scandal politician, John Profumo, and shaved his hair into an inverted Dracula's peak – the whole lot had hit the barbershop floor.

He welcomed me in and took me on a guided tour of his home, a cosy refuge lined with well-stocked bookshelves, interspersed with posters of shows, including the latest production of his one-man show *Acting Shakespeare*. I found it endearing that someone blessed with such a magnificent talent and lauded at every juncture of their career should still feel proud enough of their achievements to hang them on the wall.

Up the stairs we went to an open-plan lounge, with a magnificent view overlooking the Thames. The room was designed for comfort, a home to be lived in and to be loved. On to the top floor, and a brief glimpse of the royal bedchamber and a sumptuous *en-suite* wet room.

Returning to the lounge, my genial host opened the fridge and pulled out a bottle of *Veuve Clicquot*. A glass was poured and presented, we clinked our glasses, and I took a gentle sip of the sparkling brew, thanking my host for inviting me over.

Well, you were so attentive at the show, tending to our every need. I thought that you should be rewarded.

And with that, he took a generous swig from his glass, leaned in and shot a mouthful of champagne from his mouth into mine.

Oh my, I thought, *here's a how-de-do...*

I am in the home of one of the world's greatest actors, who has invited me over to his home for the afternoon and then for an evening at the ballet. It has just gone 3.00 pm and he has shot champagne into my mouth. Is this what the youth of today would term a 'booty call'?

What the hell do I do?
What would *you* do?

Up to this point, I had been only been with one man in my life, and I was naive enough to believe that it would last forever.

So, what *did* I do?

I was honest. I told him I was seeing someone, and that I was housesitting for a friend who was abroad, clearly implying that any thoughts of a sleepover should be dismissed.

He looked at me, with those incredibly blue and penetrating eyes, and said *Well, we've got a few hours.*

Oh...

When in times of trouble, I talk. I can talk for Britain. Pick a subject. Any subject. Let's go for the source of our meeting... Clause 28.

He grabbed the bait and we sat down, on facing sofas, and he began to talk. And talk. And talk. And it quickly became clear to me that he had only recently stepped out of the closet, and that he wanted to talk about it…a lot.

I have too often been dismissive of people in the public eye who come out after they have retired, when they will no longer have to face the potential barrage of abuse from the terraces or from the stalls. I considered their world safe and cosseted, and wondered why they had waited for a safe harbour in which to announce their 'little secret' – a supportive interview on a mid-morning chatshow, or the pages of a magazine. I understand the fear factor, of being rejected by the audience that pays your wages, but for those of us who came out on the front line, with no security guards or electronic fence to protect you, it can stir up a glass of gall.

But coming out is coming out, and he clearly wanted to talk about being gay, about the political aspects of sexuality, and his commitment to human rights and equality, and anyone who is passionate about that is more than alright in my book.

At the allotted hour, a car came to whisk us away to Islington. I became aware how immediately recognisable he was to the punters milling around outside the venue, and that we were now a figure of interest. He was surrounded by a collective of gushing thespians, who were gently pleasant and polite when introduced to the overly made-up young man standing beside the object of their attention. After a whole load of *luvvie, darling, must go, talk soon*, we were escorted into the theatre to witness the magnificence of the peerless Kirov Ballet.

In the interval, we were led to the VIP room, which was bizarre as we were the only people in there. We sipped our champagne and I thought about the nature – and the occasional loneliness – of being famous. What is the point of being ushered into a private space, far from the madding crowd of the bar, and you are the only one there? No matter how powerful, how rich, how famous you may be, at the end of everything we are all waiting for someone to find us, to look at us and say *Yep, you'll do.*

After the show, as we trundled along to the Tube in rather awkward silence, I got the distinct impression that I was in the doghouse.

I was first to disembark and I thanked him most profusely for a splendid evening, but as I stood at the platform and waved at the sullen-faced man in the departing compartment, I was aware that I had maybe not been grateful enough for the invitation or the evening.

Ah well, at least I kept my legs together.

Bent as a nine bob note

A few months later, I was called upon to provide my now well-honed backstage skills to a one-off performance of *Bent*, which would be presented at the Adelphi Theatre by an all-star cast, led by Ian McKellen.

I was requested to attend some of the later rehearsals, to acquaint myself with the running of the show, and I arrived in a room that was buzzing like a beehive. Lots of mingling, plenty of hugs and kisses, and a load of barely suppressed nerves. To stage a production in a matter of weeks was a daunting task, and the presence of such a gathering of actors would guarantee a full house, so there was no room for error.

The company included a wide-eyed Alex Jennings, the dashing Ralph Fiennes and the gauntly elegant Richard E. Grant. Tempted as I was to offer the latter a slug of lighter fluid or a toke on a Camberwell carrot, I scanned the room, saw a spare chair and staked my claim, all ready to watch the rehearsal and note down whatever was required of me to do.

The man in the next seat raised his head from his script, smiled and said *Hello*. His blonde hair was cropped short, his complexion a rather burnt red, his eyes puffy and swollen. It took a few moments to realise that I was sitting next to Ian Charleson, star of stage and screen – most notably for his appearance as Eric Liddell in *Chariots of Fire*.

The breath was stolen out of my body.

This beautiful man – who had stolen the hearts of an entire auditorium as he sang *I've Never Been In Love Before* in the legendary National Theatre production of *Guys and Dolls* –

was clearly very 'unwell', and probably dying. I had read articles and seen news reports, but this was the first time that I had ever been in such close proximity to someone living with this new and incurable disease.

There were many ridiculous myths – whipped up by fear and ignorance – about how you could contract the virus: by shaking hands, sharing a coffee cup or even a toilet seat. When nobody knows for sure, everyone becomes an expert, and rumours, fanned by the media, ran riot. Princess Diana hit the headlines when she was pictured holding hands with AIDS patients in a brave move to remove the stigma of touching someone with this still largely unknown disease. Sometimes, it's the smallest of gestures that have the greatest impact.

Charleson asked me who I was and who I was playing, and continued to be as equally charming when he learned I was a mere runner and a backstage nobody. He was cast as Greta, the supposedly straight drag queen and nightclub owner, and joked how he hoped that the heavy make-up and false eyelashes would cover up *the mess of these eyes*.

But I didn't see mess.

I saw strength battling sadness, bravery fighting fear, and determination defeating disease. As we chatted, he reached into his briefcase, pulled out a brown paper bag, reached in and produced a peach. He took a bite and gently passed it to me. For the tiniest of split seconds, the nonsense about the virus being present in saliva crossed and passed out of my mind. I took the fruit and kissed out a bite from the soft flesh, and returned it.

Maybe it meant something or nothing to him, but it meant a world to me.

McKellen spied us both and came over to say hello. He leant down and kissed Charleson on the lips and then, very tenderly, on both eyes, in a touching gesture of love and hopeful healing. They were old and good friends, both aware there would not be many more moments to share, filling the remaining time with one more memory.

As Sean Mathias, the director, called the room to order, McKellen grabbed me. Could he entrust me with the role of his own personal Man Friday for his costume changes during the show? This sounded more enjoyable than being shoved underneath the stage for the duration of the performance, so I accepted.

The day of performance began with a call to which I was to become very accustomed.

IAN...Ian wants you.

My Man Friday very swiftly became recast as Thelma Ritter. Even though he was never *going out there a nobody* and was always *gonna come back a star* that he was already, I realised that my role that day included costume changer, prop holder, tea maker, food grabber, ego masseur and occasional therapist. I was chained to the wings, on hand for any request, and only once made the mistake of straying from my post to chuck a cigarette down and look at the passing traffic on the Strand. As I returned and passed Cashman on my way back in, he informed me that McKellen was standing centre stage, bellowing out my name to the gallery.

Oh, blow wind and crack your cheeks, you big queen!

There was one particularly quick change from nightwear to a jumper, overcoat, and trouser ensemble. The rule of being dressed is that you just have to allow the dresser to do their thing. Arms up, dignity down, and let them get on with it. They know what they're doing. The worst thing you can do is struggle, do it yourself, or 'try to help'. You will simply end up fighting with each other.

During a run-through of this change, McKellen started whirling his arms like a demented windmill, laying my best-laid plans to waste. I summoned up the ghost of dear Thelma, looked him in the eye and hissed *stop it!* And like a reprimanded school boy, he did, and returned to stage and continued to do what he does best.

The show was an overwhelming success.

From the moment that poor Ben Daniels made his entrance, after standing in the wings nervously tugging every millimetre out of his penis before walking across the stage stark naked, the crowd were enraptured. Jennings was superb as the dizzy but ever-faithful Rudy. Charleson was deliciously arch as the mean-spirited Greta, crooning *Streets Of Berlin* in his glorious tenor. Cashman, although hampered by an audience who would always think of him as Colin from *Eastenders*, battled through and won as the brave and resolute Horst.

But the night belonged to McKellen. Initially boorish and lascivious, then selfish and manipulative, becoming scared, loved, loving and finally self-sacrificing. The closing moments, when he put on the jacket bearing the pink triangle that he had rejected for the entire duration of the play, and threw himself against the electric fence, his body writhing as the current coursed through him, were shocking, stunning and triumphant.

After the show, at the cast party, I stole a moment with my charge, congratulated him on a breathtaking performance, thanked him for an unforgettable experience, and produced my souvenir programme for him to sign.

He looked at me and pulled a face that said *Really? You want me to sign a programme? We've kissed! You've seen me in my pants! You want an autograph? Really??*

But I did, as a souvenir of the evening, to look at and say to myself or to others, *Look, I met Ian McKellen.*

He signed *Ian. Love Ian*, with a big kiss....
And no champagne shot to follow.

Pride in the park

Backstage of the cabaret tent at Pride 1995, and Katrina and I are getting set to entertain the troops. The area is rammed to the tent-pegs with organisers, technicians and performers, so it is mirror-to-mirror drag queens, lashing on the powder and paint before pouring themselves into something sequinned and stunning.

I always felt so plain at these events. Over the years, my onstage outfit had steadily been reduced from a shirt, tie and formal trousers to a white vest and jeans, partly for comfort in the sweaty heat of some of the venues, and partly because, hey, it's a gay crowd, let's give them a bit of flesh. Getting myself ready to go on was usually done and dusted in a matter of seconds.

But on this day of annual celebration of self, I decided to go a little bit further.

It was nearly time for our appearance, and a group of pals arrived, with McKellen in tow, all set to watch our fifteen minutes on stage. I was dressed in a long white-sleeved shirt with waistcoat, a pair of calf-length jogging pants, and *Doctor Marten* boots, looking for all the world like a *Gay City Roller*. As we were given our five-minute cue call, I removed the shirt and waistcoat, and dropped my drawers, so I was left in boots, a pair of scanty black shorts and a winning smile.

At the risk of blowing my own kazoo, I was in pretty decent shape. Years of dance classes, lugging sets and sound equipment, and a daily early morning swim had toned me up nicely. Not to the point of looking like a puffed-up poodle made out of balloons, but just enough to feel confident about going onstage wearing next to nothing.

It was as if a photographer had shouted out to the room *Hold it RIGHT THERE!*

Lipsticks stuttered to a juddering halt.
Blusher brushes froze in mid-air.
Eyelashes stopped fluttering.
Cans of hairspray were held aloft and motionless.

All you could hear was the faint tinkle of bugle beads on the fringe of a dress, the rustle of the breeze through a boa, and the faint but persistent *boom boom boom* from outside the tent. For the briefest and most beautiful moment, as every eye in the dressing area looked me up and down, and particularly down, I was the centre of attention. For one time and one time only, It was *The Boy...* and Katrina...

McKellen broke the silence with an admiring sigh and a velvet-toned purr. *Well. Everything's in the right place there.*

A few minutes later, the loud and lusty crowd who had gathered to see our set clearly and noisily agreed.

Tart that I am.

I dreamed a dream

Once upon a time, I dreamed a dream.

1975 and I was just 13, propped up in my bed reading a copy of *Disc*. The double-page centre-spread that week was a picture of Elton John, dressed with typical understatement in a sequinned baseball outfit, leaning nonchalantly on his piano and looking out at the massive audience packed into Dodgers Stadium to see him play. Tens of thousands of people cheering their adoration at a piano player.

Well, I was a piano player! And if he could...

When my mum came in to turn the lights out, I showed her the picture and said *I want that*. It took twenty years, but at Pride 95 in Victoria Park, I got it.

The Pride committee decided, after considerable pressure and protest, to acknowledge the work of the cabaret acts who did so much to entertain the community and raise money for this and many other events, by giving them a 'walk down' on the main stage.

As night fell over the park, we gathered in the holding area backstage, passing East 17 pulling a sulky pose for a photo shoot, oblivious to where they were, and waving at that cheeky Scouse songbird Sonia, who giggled and waved back.

Ian McKellen was our master of ceremonies, and was greeted onstage by a roar heard throughout the borough. He delivered a wonderful speech about the performers who get on stages in pubs and clubs up and down the country, singing their hearts out to keep spirits high and the fundraising coffers full.

As he called out the names of the raggle-taggle gang of gipsies and they clacked onto the stage in all their glamorous glory, I could hear a swell of cheering rise up from the crowd.

It was our turn. Dressed in my shorts and boots, with nipples to the evening wind, I stood behind Katrina and heard Ian introduce us.

Katrina...and the beautiful Boy.

As we stepped out from the wings, I caught a fleeting glimpse of myself on the huge video screens that hung either side of the stage. I looked out at the crowd, which went back as far as I could see, and beyond. Tiny lights in the distance danced alongside flashes from cameras. And this noise, the loudest noise I had heard this side of an aircraft on a runway. We walked forward, joined hands, bowed, and the noise got even louder...

And I thought *Well, I got here. I've no idea how. But I got here.*

We never played another Pride Festival after that day.

In 1999, Katrina and the Boy were invited to sing a musical tribute to Dusty Springfield at the *Gaytime* award ceremony, to be broadcast on television. We augmented our duo with some friends to beef up the sound, including John Springate, former vocalist and bassist with the Glitter Band, and my former band-mate and forever best-mate, Mick Williams, on guitar. We cooked up a funky little version of *Son Of A Preacher Man*, and headed to *Big Breakfast* studios to film the show.

The evening was hosted by Right Said Fred vocalist Richard Fairbrass – still looking too sexy for his shirt – and the comedienne Rhona Cameron, who made the mistake of saying over a live microphone during rehearsals that she didn't understand why they hadn't got renowned Dusty impersonator Jackie Clune to sing the tribute rather than us. Always check, people, or keep your opinion to yourself.

Among the audience were comedian Graham Norton, the model Caprice, the hot totty from *Coronation Street*, Adam Rickitt, looking absolutely terrified for most of the night, and Ian McKellen.

At the aftershow party, Ian planted a kiss on my cheek, and whispered *Best moment of the night.* He was referring to the performance, not the kiss, I might add.

We were now officially good friends.

The wizard and I

The new millennium was a time of great change for both the Ians in this story. I became a secondary-school drama teacher, and he conquered the world in two of the biggest blockbusters of all time, playing Magneto in *X-Men* and delivering his legendary performance as Gandalf in the epic *Lord of the Rings* trilogy.

Well, you do what you do.

One day an email arrived on my desk with a simple but irresistible offer. *Would you like Gandalf to fly in on his broomstick and meet your children?*

McKellen's dedication to breaking down homophobic barriers and carrying the banner for human rights and equality was renowned, and he had recently begun a series of visits to secondary-schools to throw his support behind the fight against the daily bullying some gay schoolchildren have to endure on the playground.

The rise in use of computers and mobile phones, and the popularity of social media, chatrooms, and texting had led to a horrific increase in cyber-bullying and teenage suicide, with aggressors spreading their poison from behind a protective screen of anonymity, reaching their audience with the minimum of effort and devastating consequences.

I was not prepared to let that happen.
Not on my watch.
Not in my school.

While the kids in my charge were no more ignorant nor less informed than any other of their generation, the rise in popularity of rap stars like Eminem had given them an unfortunate new language of bigotry. The traditional playground taunts of *queer* and *poofter* were now augmented by *batty boy* and *faggot*, and the word *gay* itself had became an insult, synonymous with something weak, perverted and wrong. My day would be regularly punctuated with reprimanding a child for misuse of the word, and became the catalyst for an assembly to remind the student body that sticks and stones may break your bones, but words can break your heart.

With the aid of the media department and a dedicated crew of Sixth Formers, I created a video collage of famous gay men and lesbians who had made an invaluable contribution to the world. It was fascinating to observe the faces of the students as they watched a procession of emperors and queens, authors and sportswomen, singers and television stars, men and women who left an indelible footprint on the planet, and yet had been forced to conceal the light of their love for too many years.

At the heart of the assembly was a brief but powerful account of the appalling murder of Matthew Shephard, a young man kidnapped, beaten and left to die tied to a fence in a field in Laramie, Wyoming. I concluded the presentation by asking the students if they really wanted to use the hate-filled language that were probably the last words that Matthew ever heard on this earth, and invited them to consider the damage they do by using homophobic language whilst sitting next to someone who, unbeknownst to them, had a gay brother or sister, a gay uncle or aunt, a gay mother or father, or might be gay themselves.

I like to hope and believe that they got the message.

I wanted to keep McKellen's visit to the school as quiet as possible. The presence of a major movie star was going to cause huge interest across the 1600-strong student body, most of whom were obsessed by celebrity, and I decided that he should spend some 'quiet time' with the A-level drama students, before doing a question and answer audience with the eighty-strong GCSE consortium. A brief interview and photo session with the school newspaper and the day would be done.

When I told the students he was coming, I sensed mild disbelief in the room. It was easy for them to be cynical. *Why on earth would an A-list film actor come to Welling? Nothing like that ever happens in Welling.* But they duly wrote down their questions to ensure the forum section of the day did not descend into a verbal bunfight, and the countdown was on.

As Gandalf, Magneto, and Sir Ian McKellen walked into their classroom, wrapped inside a big black coat and wearing a very dapper hat, their eyes grew as big as their smiles, and there was a communal gasp as he ceremoniously produced a huge sword that he had kept as a souvenir of Middle Earth, along with a clapperboard from the set of *X-Men*. He placed the relics on a table, smiled at the assembled company, and began to talk, instantly putting them at their ease, speaking *to* them and *with* them rather than *at* them, and they responded with a series of intelligent questions, which he answered with quite disarming honesty.

Within the first ten minutes he laid his cards on the table. *I only really know about two things. One is being an actor, and the other is being a gay man, and one of those I have been all my life.* He answered questions about what it was like doing love scenes with women, about whether he had ever fancied any of his co-stars, what he thought of Orlando Bloom, indeed what he thought about everything and anything. As he spoke, curled up in his chair, looking more like a dishevelled uncle at a family party than one of the most famous actors in the world, the students listened intently and without interruption, which in itself was no small miracle.

At one point, a member of the audience asked how we had met. I threw him a look, silently pleading with him not to tell the champagne shot story. While I was now 'out' to both staff and students, a girl's got to have some secrets. I grabbed the baton and reminded him of our Clause 28 and Stonewall connection, which provided a merciful detour and meant that I would not forever be thought of by my classes as Gandalf's booty call.

One of the students asked him to do a line from *Lord of the Rings*, which he declined with a laugh and mumbled excuse. But, about ten minutes later, when he had risen from his seat to make a particular point, and with no warning, he looked at the lad from a few feet away and bellowed down at him *YOU SHALL NOT PASS!* The boy's shocked face rippled at the sheer force of that voice, as if he was flying around a roller coaster at top speed. He won't forget that in a hurry.

Ian announced that he was going to conclude the session with a little-known speech from the play *Sir Thomas More*, written in part by William Shakespeare. He had selected an emotional speech from a scene where More – sent by the King to quell a riot on the streets of London, where an angry crowd are demanding that *strangers* be removed – makes a poignant plea for greater acceptance in the face of violence and ignorance.

From the first word, the dishevelled uncle disappeared like dust in the wind. Here was the actor, his voice full, resonant, filling every corner of the room, eyes blazing with passion and burning into those of the wonderstruck audience. Each sentence aimed straight for their hearts, questioning, imploring, each word laced with rage and disbelief that human beings could treat their fellow members of the human race with such *'momtainish inhumanity'*.

As the last words echoed round the darkened space of the drama studio, everything seemed to stop. Time. Breath. Life itself. Just for a second. Then the applause broke out, as the audience rose as one. It was quite a moment for them, me, and hopefully for him.

The bell rang to announce lunch, but no-one seemed in a particular hurry to leave. One boy came up, with his school planner, and asked for an autograph, followed by another, and another. A queue formed and he signed every single book. As one of my most dedicated drama students passed me on his way out, his face a picture of joy and disbelief, he gasped *He looked straight at me, Sir. Like, right at me.* I smiled as he left on his own particular cloud nine, and I imagined his response that evening to the traditional parental teatime question

So, anything happen at school today?
Yeah. I met Gandalf.

After the room was cleared, and some semblance of quiet returned to the corridors, I walked our guest through to the relative sanctuary of the conference room, where he would be interviewed by the school press gang. As we made our way, two twelve-year-old boys, late for a lesson, ran towards and past us. We heard the squeak of soles and one ran back, looked McKellen in the face, and shouted to his mate *It IS him! I told you!* prompting Sir Ian to laugh and mutter *Hobbits.*

At the press conference, the table was covered with plates of sandwiches and bowls of crisps, none of which were touched by the awestruck group of students. McKellen sat at the head of the table, and willingly answered every question put to him, taking every opportunity to push forward the Stonewall message of learning tolerance, showing acceptance, embracing the gay and lesbian members of the school community, and ending homophobic bullying.

Sitting next to him was a first year student with an immaculately combed pudding-basin haircut and cherubic face, clearly overwhelmed by the presence of the great man sitting next to him.

Each time McKellen took a few crisps, he gently pushed the bowl a little closer in the young lad's direction, silently and subtly encouraging him to tuck in and share the snack, not dissimilar to the scene in *War Horse*, when Albert is making friends with Joey, the timid young foal. Inch by inch, eyes not meeting, without a word, but bit by bit, the bowl was moved across the table, until eventually a young hand reached in and took a crisp. And then another.

I hope he still had room for his tea, and, if he didn't, he had a good story to tell as to why he was full up.

By the time the day was nearly done, word had gone round the school, and the windowed door of the conference room became a spy hole for passing staff, all slowing their traditional breakneck walk between class and staffroom to have a quick look and move on.

All except one bible-thumping member of the Religious Education department, who had talked to me daily until he found out that I was *the spawn of Beelzebub*. He burst into the room, without invitation or warning, and moved purposefully towards McKellen.

Oh my God! I thought, quickly scanning the intruder for a string of garlic and a wooden stake, *he's going to kill him!*

But no, he just wanted a selfie.

Without so much as a *by-your-leave*, he leant in, put his arm around McKellen's shoulder, took the picture and left the room.

I would have paid good money to witness the moment when someone broke the news and told him he had just hugged a big homo. That will be two *Hail Marys*, a week in sacking and stilettos, and a quick chorus of *Don't Rain On My Parade!*

That'll teach you.

I've been to a marvellous party

Almost twenty years after first knocking at McKellen's front door, I was there again, this time on his kind invitation to attend a New Year's Eve party.

I was greeted at the door by our glamorous host, resplendent in a flowing blue shirt and a pair of patchwork leather trousers, and was led into a reception area already alive with people whose last names I already knew.

Hello to Simon (Callow), hello to Patrick (Stewart) and hello dear to Steven (Berkoff), dressed in a blue and silver-trimmed nehru jacket, with matching pointed shoes, looking for all the world like the evil vizier in *Aladdin*. I was introduced as a school-teacher, prompting an *oooh* from the assembled thespians, as they wondered if they had worked with me at the National. Ian briefly described his visit to my workplace, and I was as proud of his account as he was to tell it.

Left alone to mingle, I grabbed a glass of something sparkling and found myself in conversation with Patrick Stewart – no hardship as I could listen to his dulcet tones all day and night. I told him how strange it was to be talking to him in the flesh, as I had spent the last week of the term winding my classes down for the festive season with showings of his appearance as Scrooge in *A Christmas Carol*.

I told him that, in all honesty and having watched many versions of this famous tale, I thought his version was the best, and for the next ten minutes, he agreed with me. Well, it's Christmas and if you can't toot your own horn at this time of celebration, when can you? When he finally stopped, I – like a fool – said the performance of his that I really enjoyed was his superb performance as an A-grade New York queen in the small-budget classic gay movie *Jeffery*. His face lit up and, for another ten minutes, he agreed with me. He even admitted to watching it at home sometimes, and reeled off some of his favourite lines, which I was only too happy to hear repeated up close and personal.

Me: *Who's Anne Miller?*
Him: *Leave this house.*

Marvellous.

Before we could move onto his interpretation of *Macbeth*, which I had seen, and his Captain Pickard, which I hadn't, our conversation was joined by a lovely lady who launched into a rambling remembrance of *auld Ireland*. I am ashamed to say that I did not recognise her and had to be subtly informed by my host that she was the doyenne of Irish literature, Edna O'Brien.

Well, you can't know everybody.

The doorbell kept ringing and guests kept arriving. Anthony Cotton, who was as lovely as I had hoped, and Russell Tovey, who was sexier than I had expected. The playwright Martin Sherman, whom I had not seen since that performance of *Bent*, was also in attendance, and I took the opportunity to tell him that I was working on Act One of his most famous play with my final year A-Level students. He looked aghast, clutching an imaginary pearl necklace and saying *Really? You're doing it with KIDS?* I invited him to follow in McKellen's footsteps by coming to the school and having a chat with the cast. He looked vaguely interested, but that sadly never happened. I wish he could have seen the final performance, as they nailed it.

Midnight approached, and the guests assembled to charge their glasses and prepared to sing in the New Year. As *Big Ben* chimed and fireworks exploded and lit up the London skyline, I added my shy little whisper to the most vocally perfect rendition of *Auld Lang Syne* I have ever heard, and smiled with contentment as the magnificent chorus of open vowels and clipped consonants echoed across the Thames.

Within the hour, I was making my leave. My genial host put his arm around my shoulders, surveyed the kitchen packed with guests and whispered *Do you know, darling, I have no idea who half these people are.* And maybe he didn't. There will always be those who manage to slide in on the shirttails of a friend of a friend of a friend, and spend the next week telling everyone who will listen that they spent New Year's Eve partying with Ian McKellen.

Funny old world.

I thanked Ian for including me in the evening and we hugged and kissed farewell before I headed out into the night. Walking slightly tipsy down the cobbled street, the sky lit by stars and the occasional firework, the water gently lapping against the riverbank, it did fleetingly cross my mind that if time and circumstance had been different, I could have been Lady Ian McKellen.

But I am more than happy and proud to call him my friend.

Like father, like son

The day I met
my dad

Daddy, my daddy

When I was seven years old, I asked my father to buy me a tutu. He kindly but firmly refused, which is a shame, as I think I would have worn it well.

Mind you, I blame him.

My first theatrical experience was a family outing to see *The Sleeping Beauty* at the Royal Opera House when I was six years old. As I was led down the aisle, I gazed up and around in awe and wonder at the layered tiers of this majestic building. Balconies of white and gold, crowned by the dizzying heights of the amphitheatre and an enormous chandelier. And everywhere, lights, lights, twinkling lights.

I sat on the red plush seat, in my little corduroy shorts, with my sandalled feet swinging over the edge, gazing at the huge, heavy, red velvet curtains, embossed with the initials *ER* in gold, watching as the orchestra pit began to fill with black-jacketed and bow-tied musicians, who settled and started to tune up, sending this mysterious eerie sound over the stalls and up to the gods.

The conductor emerged to applause from the rows of suits and sable, and the lights dimmed as the overture began.

Bows hit strings, kettle drums rolled, cymbals crashed and trumpets blew, as the curtains rose and parted to reveal a fairytale palace, all brilliant white and dazzling gold. Courtiers in elaborate hats and frock coats filled the stage, joined by ladies-in-waiting, elegantly gliding across the boards in voluminous ballgowns and glittering tiaras, sailing on the waves of romantic melodies...

And that was when the bug bit. From that moment, I decided that my life would be beautiful, glamorous, magical and set to music.

Listening to music with my Dad is a favourite shared moment of my childhood.

An opera fanatic, he believed in doing his homework to fully appreciate the piece, and would arm himself with both the weighty *Companion to Opera* and the libretto, place the record in the stereogram and the needle on the vinyl, before settling on the sofa to listen, read and inwardly digest.

I would sit beside him, listening to these wonderful sounds, with passionate arias sung in an unintelligible language, and to his responses when I asked what on earth was happening. I would contentedly hold the record cover, gazing at the imperious face of Maria Callas as *Tosca*, resplendent in her red velvet gown, and demanding every five minutes *Is she dead yet?* before dramatically hurling myself off the castle-walled sofa and striking a suitably fractured pose on the carpet floor. Viva la Diva.

My saddest memory of my father from my childhood years is that he was so often away on business for his firm of solicitors, making frequent trips to the Philippines, Egypt and Greece. I missed him, and counted the days until he returned, especially if the length of time away was compensated by a small gift from the country he had visited.

Even at home, he always seemed to be working.

Every Saturday and Sunday morning, the whole house was locked into a church-like silence, so that he could wade his way through mountains of paperwork, and in the afternoons he would don an ancient pair of trousers and tend his beloved garden.

His years at public school, university and Royal Marines had instilled an innate desire for order and organisation, timetabling each moment of his life, and his upbringing as the sole son of a stern father and a demanding mother had made him a dutiful – if emotionally formal – man.

I learned from my mother that his proposal of marriage was accompanied by a list of income and outgoings, and her arrival at the altar on their wedding day was greeted with the hopelessly unromantic *Well done, you're on time.*

But in my eyes, he was a leading man in every film I saw. He was Robin Hood, taking from the rich to give to the poor, Caractacus Potts, making a broken-down car fly, and Captain Von Trapp, learning how to love his children by singing a song about edelweiss.

He was my hero. He was *Daddy, my Daddy.*

As my first school reports showed a complete failure to understand the work-ings of Mathematics, he tried his hand at some home tutoring, using pieces of *Mars Bars* to explain multiplication and division, but all to no avail, and my failure to understand was increasingly interpreted as stupidity laced with an unhealthy dash of laziness.

The quiet but colourful rebellion during my adolescence, combined with my inability to appreciate the privilege of my time at Cheltenham College, let alone achieve any notable academic success, only added to the bubbling cauldron of antagonism brewing between us, and my latter teenage years saw my relationship with my father disintegrate from luke-warm to cold to frozen.

In my early twenties, we could barely be in the same room as each other, our nightly confrontations over the dinner table heralded with his cutting opening line of *What have you done today that I would approve of?* and usually parried by my surly *Probably nothing.* If we were lucky, we would get through the next twenty minutes without another word. If more were spoken, they were inevitably a vitriolic attack on my directionless existence, my lack of a clear career path, and anything else that came to mind.

I was left in no doubt that I was a total disappointment, and I equated this with my assumption that he had not only sussed out that I was gay, but whole-heartedly disapproved.

On one occasion, as he caught me heading out of the door to a Hollywood-themed 21st birthday party, dressed as Marlon Brando in *The Wild Ones*, a vision in black leather from Muir-capped head to booted toe, he sliced me with a crisp *You know what you look like, don't you?*

Yes, I did know, and clearly he did too.

An uneasy ceasefire was declared when I got into drama school, and my visits to the family home became reduced to less than a week spread over an entire year, including the decidedly joyless family Christmas, where we set a record for sitting down to lunch, eating, clearing away and returning to the living room in fifty minutes.

We never kissed, hugged hello, or even touched, apart from one singular moment in a church when I patted his arm after he returned to the pew having struggled through the final sentence of a eulogy to his eldest sister.

But the shouting and arguing had mercifully stopped, despite the fact that my appearance was now an open broadcast to the world that I very definitely was what I was. We would talk about the shows that we had seen, or the work that I was doing, and I felt that he was quietly proud of the fact that I was living my life and pursuing my dream of being an entertainer of some sort.

One day, my home phone rang, and it was my Dad, which was unheard of in itself. He never called. Ever. *I have some tickets for the Phillip Glass opera 'Akhenaten', if you would like to come.*

David Bowie liked Phillip Glass, therefore I liked Phillip Glass, so the answer was an absolute yes.

Good. I have a ticket for you and one for a friend, and I will be bringing someone who your mother mustn't know about.

It was a line worthy of an *Eastenders* drum beat.

As I put the phone down, I wondered who this person might be. A work colleague from the office? My mother was vociferous in her poor opinion of some of Dad's work partners and the massive demands they put upon him, so it could be one of them. We shall see.

I arrived at the restaurant in St Martin's Lane, my Dad's traditional feeding place before heading down to the nearby Coliseum. We had eaten there many times over the years as a family, in both good and bad times, and there was thus nothing remarkable or secretive about the choice of venue.

My companion for the evening was Sally, my voice teacher from drama college, a very good friend and one who I knew would enjoy the challenging music of Mr Glass. My Dad arrived and the three of us sat around the table, making small talk and waiting for the final member of the party.

The door opened, and in walked this young Asian man in his late twenties. On seeing my Dad, he came over and joined us at the table. He was bespectacled, immaculately dressed in a black velvet jacket, and wearing a ring on every finger. As he sat down, my father introduced him as Rudy, with no explanation as to who he was. Nothing.

Menus were passed around, food was selected and served, wine was poured and conversation ensued. Not that I can remember a single word. I was having a much more interesting conversation under the table, my knee tapping out Morse Code messages of confusion to Sally.

As we ate, I watched in wide-eyed disbelief as Rudy passed some of his food onto my Dad's plate, without the flicker of an eyelash from either of them.

Cue more frantic knee knocking.

After the meal, we headed down to the Coliseum and Dad handed over our tickets. We were not sitting together, but we *were* invited to join them at the interval for a drink. Sally and I found our seats, sat down and paused for thought.

I went first...

Well, I said.
Well, she said.

And that was all we said.

Neither my father nor I made any mention of this evening for the next two years, until we had to have a business meeting at his office.

It was 1989, and I was desperate to purchase a home of my own, having had enough of living in rented accommodation as a student and then as a fledgling actor, which was merely serving to line the pocket of some greedy landlord. I was now earning enough to support mortgage repayments, but the initial deposit required was too far out of reach.

My wayward boyfriend had made the heart-lifting proposal that we should buy a place together. Buoyed by bluebirds, stupidly hoping that this was the overture for a happy life of living together, I spoke to Dad and he stated that he was prepared to help us out, not only financially, but also by spiriting some of the legal fees into the ether.

We met at his office in Bishopsgate and I felt decidedly nervous as the clock ticked towards the hour of our appointment. We sat and talked, as I showed him pictures of the property – which required a lot of redecoration – in a perfect location and affordable. He noted the necessary figures, did the sums, and said he would assist me. I was absolutely over the moon.

He then sat back in his chair. *Right. Now, let's talk about the politics of all this. How much does your mother know about this relationship?*

I felt my insides tighten. I had not foreseen this.

Well, she knows I've got a friend called Gary, I responded, cagily.

I see. And is that all she knows?
Yes, I said, hoping to leave it there, but the silence that followed dashed that hope against the rocks.

I breathed in, exhaled, and looked him in the eye.

Obviously you know more.
Yes, I think I do.

And I found myself doing what I had never done before, when it came to the matter of my sexuality.

I apologised.

I'm sorry.
Why are you sorry?
I thought you would be angry.
Why should I be angry?
I thought you would be disappointed.
Why should I be disappointed?

I had nowhere left to go.

How did you know? When did you know? I asked, as if dogs in the street didn't know I was gay.

Well, I'm a man of the world. That's why I wanted you to meet Rudy.

The book of secrets was open. He told me the story of how they met. Showed me a watercolour on his desk that Rudy had painted for him. Told me of how they had been holidaying in Rudy's home country of Singapore, and how – as they were coming through customs – the officials had let him through, but not Rudy. That they had confiscated Rudy's passport and never returned it. How they wrote to each other every week, just as he had written to me when I was at Cheltenham College.

I am sure that he told me a lot more, but there was only so much I could absorb, and maybe more than I thought I could hear. But I do remember leaving his office, turning left and walking, not knowing where I was going. Just walking and trying to make sense of what I had just heard.

I couldn't make any sense of it at all.

We never spoke about that conversation again.
Nor about Rudy.
Ever.

Over the next decade, our relationship steadily improved, and when I was working on the gay cabaret circuit, Dad decided that he wanted to come along and watch a performance at *Manhattans* in Earls Court, one of the more respectable dives where we used to ply our trade.

He sat at a corner table with my brother – the latter with his head in his hands for most of the evening – gently smiling as he watched me bump and grind out a song about sado-masochism to a very enthusiastic audience of check-shirted queens, and even came backstage to voice his appreciation of the show, *and* backed it up with a congratulatory phone call the next day.

Peace was officially declared. We were friends. Better friends, maybe, than we were as father and son, and with much more in common than most.

A few years later, as I was finishing my first half term as a teacher, I called to say I would be visiting the family home. Dad and I had our typically brief conversation before he passed the phone to my mother, but I could hear an undertone of pride in his bemusement that his academic dunce of a son was now a teacher.

It was the last time we spoke.

On the morning of February 16 2001, my father got out of bed, got dressed and went downstairs. He sat in his chair, suffered an aneurism and died.

Driving home, barely able to see the road for tears, my mind was a kaleidoscope of memories.

The good, the bad.
The beautiful, and the ugly.

As I sat with my mother in his study, the room where he had died, I noticed a picture frame on his desk, holding a picture of me and Donny Osmond, my childhood hero. I smiled, shaking my head, and said *I can't believe he has that up.*

She replied, *Oh, that was one of his most prized possessions. He would show it off to anyone who came into the house.*

The things we never know...

At his funeral, I stood beside my brother and mother, and the priest invited us to take a moment for our own personal reflections...and I had a raging argument with my father in my head.

All the *why why whys*, those now unanswerable questions that had meant everything but now meant nothing.

As the seconds passed, I was aware the minister would interrupt my thoughts and the chance would be gone and lost forever, so I'd better say it now.

It's OK.

Just in time.

But if I had five more minutes with my Dad, maybe I would ask him...

Did you always know you were gay?
Did you marry my mother for love?
For duty? For children?
For respectability?
Were all those lost years of anger between us rooted in your resentment that I was living a life that you had to deny and hide?

But then again, maybe I wouldn't.

Maybe I would find a better use for those five minutes.

Like thanking him for everything.
And telling him that I love him.

Yes. That'll do.

From there to here

The day I met
you

I never meant to write a book

Over the years, I told many of the tales you have just read to anyone who would listen, and had grown contentedly used to hearing *You should write a book*, safe in the knowledge that I never would.

But having taken early retirement from teaching, freeing myself from the high-speed insanity of a secondary school, I had time to reflect on what I had done with my life, where I was and where I was hopefully heading.

What began as a ticklish gossip about celebrities became a tribute to my personal icons and heroes and – finally – an acknowledgement of my milestones in the hard-fought journey since the 1967 Wolfenden Report ended years of arrests and prosecutions by recommending that

> *homosexual behaviour between consulting adults in private should no longer be a criminal offence.*

Milestones.

Singing that I was glad to be gay, marching alongside the miners at Gay Pride, protesting against Clause 28, witnessing the devastation of HIV/AIDS, and flying the rainbow flag in the name of Stonewall and equality.

This is our history and we need to acknowledge, applaud, protect and share it.

Every time we forget our gay brothers, lesbian sisters,

bisexuals and transgenders who marched, chanted, demonstrated and fought for the right to love and live as absolute equals, we disrespect their contribution to our present freedom.

Every time a drag queen takes her final bow and leaves this earthly stage, we laugh a little less and our world loses a little more of that glitz and glamour that we have always turned to in the darkest of times.

Every time the door closes on another iconic gay venue, it is more than the portraits, photographs and posters that get locked away, out of sight and slowly out of mind. There are the spirits of those we miss, the songs we sang, the dances we did, the fun and fisticuffs, the laughter, the lust, the tears, and all that celebration, all that love.

If memories are not shared, our lives become like lost tombs, a trove of priceless treasures gathering dust.

Forgotten.

Maya Angelou said *You can't really know where you going until you know where you have been*, and she is never wrong.

Looking back, from there to here, I realise that I have been a lot braver than I thought I was and think I am.

It took guts to be the only Osmond fan on the playground, to be the painted peacock of my public school, to stand onstage in front of the toughest audiences on the planet and to be an *out* gay teacher, and I could not have done any of it without someone, be they famous or friend, to lead me on.

So, my gratitude to every musician, actor, writer and artist who thrilled and inspired me to explore my own imagination.

To every teacher who taught me not only their subject, but how to love the never-ending path of learning.

To every performer who shared both stage and spotlight, with a particular bow to Katrina for ten wonderful years of mad adventure.

To every student who made me realise that the applause you hear for others is infinitely sweeter than the round you hear for yourself.

To every lover who – for however long – made me breathe out, relax, and feel like the war was over.

To everyone who encouraged me to pursue and complete this project, with special thanks to Steve Pottinger, poet, editor *extraordinaire* and the beating heart of Ignite Books, without whom this book would still be sitting in a drawer.

To my family of friends on both sides of Atlantic…you are my heroes.

And to you for reading.

I xx

I've been to a marvellous party
With Bowie and Walters and Wood
Two Georges, one Jimmy, a Liza Minnelli
With Donny and Stritchy and Cook
Maupin and Robinson, Curry and Crisp
Savage and sweet Ian Mckellen
They sang to me, spoke to me
Showed me the way
To learn and to shout
That it's great to be gay
And as dear Noel Coward would so sweetly say
I couldn't have liked it more!

also from Ignite Books

Kiss & Make up

by

Carl Stanley

'A great ride. Raw, messy, sometimes a laugh, sometimes a heartbreaker, usually wildly over-dressed, this first-person tale of survival is a bit like the pop-haunted decades it whirls us back into – years when being a young queer took a lot of nerve as well as a lot of eyeliner.'

Neil Bartlett – playwright, director, performer and writer

'Carl Stanley is a natural born writer. Whatever else he is, I couldn't possibly comment. You'll just have to read his highly entertaining memoir and find out for yourself!'

Paul Burston – author and founder of 'Polari' literary salon

available at **www.ignitebooks.co.uk**

Ignite Books is a small, independent publisher. This book is the latest in our series which we hope puts thought-provoking, entertaining writing before a new audience. We have a lot of fun doing this, but we also survive on a shoestring budget and a lot of graft. So, if you've enjoyed this book, please tell your friends about us. You can also find us on twitter, so drop by and say hallo. And to learn more about what we do, or to shop for our other publications, you'll find our website at

ignitebooks.co.uk

Thank you.